Against the New Authoritarianism

AGAINST
THE NEW AUTHORITARIANISM

Politics

After

Abu Ghraib

HENRY GIROUX

Arbeiter Ring Publishing •Winnipeg

Copyright © Henry A. Giroux 2005
Arbeiter Ring Publishing
201E-121 Osborne St.
Winnipeg, Manitoba
Canada R3L 1Y4
www.arbeiterring.com

Printed in Canada.
Cover image "Critical Mass" by Antony Gormley. Copyright © the artist. Courtesy of the artist and Jay Jopling/White Cube.

With assistance of the Manitoba Arts Council/Conseil des Arts du Manitoba.
We acknowledge the support of the Canada Council for the Arts for our publishing program.

MANITOBA arts COUNCIL   Canada Council   Conseil des Arts
CONSEIL DES ARTS DU MANITOBA   for the Arts   du Canada

Library and Archives Canada Cataloguing in Publication
    Giroux, Henry A.
    Against the new authoritarianism : politics after Abu-Ghraib / Henry A. Giroux.
ISBN 1-894037-23-5
    1. Authoritarianism--United States. 2. United States--Politics and government--2001-. 3. Abu Ghraib Prison. 4. Democracy--United States.
5. Religious fundamentalism--United States. I. Title.

For Zygmunt Bauman
whose intelligence, political convictions, and courage
embody what it means to struggle for a more just and democratic world.

For Nasrin Rahimieh
a courageous visionary and a symbol of hope in dark times.

For Susan Searls Giroux
my one and only love.

Contents

Acknowledgments

This book is part of a dialogue I have been having for some time about the growing authoritarianism emerging in the United States under the administration of George W. Bush. While I have always been very cautious about using the word authoritarianism, I believe the conditions of oppression that are occurring both domestically and abroad because of policies promoted by the United States demand more than the vocabulary of a somewhat disturbed and unsettled liberalism. Those of us fighting for global democracy and justice need a new language, sense of rage, and passion to endure, resist, and organize against the dreadful machinery of death, exploitation, fundamentalism, and moral indifference that now drives American politics. This book was largely written and revised soon after I left the US to live and work in Canada. With a war raging abroad and on the domestic front, Susan Searls Giroux and I decided to leave the United States and take new jobs at McMaster University. Largely leaving the US because of a wonderful job opportunity and feeling the despair of living in a country that is attacking every vestige of democracy, I now write from a position that offers some security and protection, but not without a sense of homelessness and displacement. While this type of move is always difficult, it has been made much easier for me and Susan as a result of a number of friends, including Liss Platt, Jasmin Habib, Janice Hldaki, Imre Szeman, Maria Whiteman, Nasrin Rahimieh, Ken Norrie, and Lorna Higdon-Norrie, Mary O'Connor, David Clark, Tracy Wynne, Roger and Wendy Simon, and too many others to mention. I purposely wanted to publish this book with an independent press in the hopes that doing so would be consistent with the democratic principles that informed it. For letting me do that, I want to thank my editor, Todd Scarth. Thanks also to copy editor Pat Sanders, proofreader Carolynn Smallwood, and Noeline Bridge, who prepared the index. My deepest gratitude to my graduate research assistants at McMaster University: Grace Pollock and Jake Kennedy, who read endless drafts of the manuscript and helped greatly to improve it. I also want to thank my administrative assistant, Maya Stamenkovic, for her amazing skills, support, warmth, and friendship. Antoinette Somo has also provided great support in helping me adjust to McMaster University. Lastly, I want to thank my brilliant, compassionate, and supportive partner, Susan Searls Giroux.

Some of the ideas in these chapters are drawn from work published in other places. Parts of Chapter One were published in a much different form as a Phi Delta Kappa monograph. Parts of Chapter Two first appeared in *Cultural Studies* 18,16 (November, 2004): 779-815. And Chapter Three first appeared in *Tikkun* 19,6 (November-December 2004): 62-64.

INTRODUCTION: BETRAYING DEMOCRACY

The events of September 11th hastened a major shift not only in domestic and foreign policy, but also "in our nation's self-understanding. It became commonplace to refer to an 'American Empire' and to the United States as 'the world's only superpower.'"[1] Embracing a policy moulded largely by fear and bristling with partisan, right-wing ideological interests, the Bush administration took advantage of the tragedy of 9/11 by adopting and justifying a domestic and foreign policy that blatantly privileged security over freedom, the rule of the market over social needs, and militarization over human rights and social justice. Multilateralism in foreign affairs gave way to unilateralism and a disregard for international law, fuelled by a foreign policy that defined itself through the arrogance of unbridled power. Refusing to ratify a number of landmark international agreements such as the Antiballistic Missile Treaty, the International Criminal Court, and the Kyoto Protocol, the Bush administration increasingly displayed an "insulting arrogance toward the United Nations in general, and individual members in particular."[2] National security was now delineated as part of a larger policy in which the United States had the right to use preventive military force "to eliminate a perceived threat, even if invented or imagined."[3] Senator Byrd described the unprecedented Bush doctrine of pre-emptive strike as an irresponsible policy that sets a dangerous precedent, undermines Congress's constitutional authority to declare war, and produces a "rising tide of anti-Americanism across the globe."[4] Global hegemony now became synonymous with national security as official policy proclaimed that any challenge to United States power and supremacy would be blocked by military force.[5] After the attack on Afghanistan, American forces invaded Iraq, an invasion justified through what later was proved to be a series of blatantly misleading arguments by the Bush administration.[6] Moreover, far from making the country safer, many foreign policy analysts, including Gareth Evans, former Australian foreign minister, argued that the invasion of Iraq only served to convince many people in the Arab world that the United States was more intent on humiliating the Islamic world than on bringing "democracy" to Iraq. Such actions on the part of the Bush administration have not only unified Islamic terrorists, but have also created a greater threat to Americans at home and abroad, especially to those soldiers and personnel serving in Iraq and Afghanistan. As Evans puts it, "The unhappy truth is that the net result of the war on terror, so far at least, has been more war and more terror."[7]

"Empire" soon became the requisite term to define American power abroad. What has become clear since the invasion of Iraq is the willingness of the Bush administration to wage a war on terrorism at the expense of civil liberties, just as it scrapped a foreign policy that at least made a gesture towards democratic values for one that unleashes untold violence in the name of combating evil and exercising control over all other global powers. As Robert Jay Lifton points out, war has now taken on a mythic and heroic status under the Bush administration, "carried out for the defense of one's nation, to sustain its special historical destiny and the immortality of its people."[8] Such a doctrine is far from heroic, resulting in widespread fear, anxiety, massive suffering, and death, but also undermining the credibility of the American government as a bastion of democracy. The pictures of US soldiers humiliating and torturing Iraqi detainees at Abu Ghraib, the charge by the International Committee of the Red Cross that torture was used on prisoners at Guantanamo Bay, Cuba, and the more recent revelations that prisoners were tortured and killed in Bagram prison in Afghanistan have drawn strong reactions in the Arab media and around the world. They have also largely undermined any moral and political credibility on the part of the US government to defend its actions in Iraq. What, in fact, has been described as a war for freedom and democracy in Iraq by the Bush administration is now largely viewed by Muslims and Arabs all over the world as an attack on Islamic culture, especially in light of recent revelations by prisoners at Abu Ghraib and Guantanamo Bay that female interrogators smeared them with menstrual blood and assaulted them sexually. Increasingly, the United States war on terrorism has been viewed at home and abroad as a continuation of the very terrorism it attempts to eliminate.

AGAINST THE NEW AUTHORITARIANISM

On the domestic front, a strange mixture of neo-conservative ideologues, free-market right-wingers, and evangelical Christians began to wage another kind of war, this one against the social contract that had been put in place by Franklin Delano Roosevelt's New Deal and Lyndon Johnson's Great Society, but also against the longstanding division between the church and state, between secular reason and religious beliefs. The needs of poor, working-class, and middle-class Americans are now under siege by the Bush administration, which instituted tax cuts for the richest 1 percent, increased corporate welfare, bankrolled a massive military machine, and turned a 2001 government surplus of $127 billion into a deficit of $400 billion by 2006.[9] In short, public assets have been hijacked by those at the top of the economic pyramid, leaving few public resources for financially strapped state and local governments to use to address new problems or long-term improvements. One specific—and intended—outcome of this policy is that there is very little money or assistance available for those Americans most in need. The rich get tax handouts and corporate relief, while the most basic healthcare services for children, the elderly, and the disabled are either cut or dramatically reduced.[10] For example, "about 270,000 children of low-income, working parents have been barred from health insurance programs in the nine states where estimates are available."[11] The Center on Budget and Policy Priorities reports that, with thirty-four states making cuts over the last few years in public health insurance programs, "Some 1.2 million to 1.6 million low-income people—including 490,000 to 650,000 children and large numbers of parents, seniors, and people with disabilities—have lost publicly funded health coverage as a result."[12] Over 37 percent of all children lack health insurance in the world's wealthiest nation. Paul Krugman calls Bush's latest budget projections a form of class warfare since he "takes food from the mouths of babes and gives the proceeds to his millionaire friends."[13] In his 2006 budget proposals, Bush calls for terminating aid for over 300,000 people receiving food stamps, and denies child-care assistance to over 300,000 children from working-class families while, at the same time, phasing out a limit on tax exemptions for high-income families that would give taxpayers with incomes over $1 million an average tax cut of more than $19,000.[14] In this case, savage cuts in education, nutritional assistance for impoverished mothers, veterans' medical care, and basic scientific research help fund tax cuts for the inordinately rich. Under President Bush's 2006 budget, the long-standing social contract central to American democracy is not simply deteriorating; it is under sustained attack by free-market extremists and Christian right-wingers. In what is truly one of the most glaring contradictions of the current Republican-led government, vast numbers of people are now being severed by the Bush administration from the most basic social provisions and public resources at the same time that Bush and his aids are increasingly using the hyped-up language of religious morality and "compassionate conservatism" to defend the discourse of free-market fundamentalism and a politics that largely caters to the rich and powerful. Congressman Bernie Sanders, in an exchange with FED Chairman Alan Greenspan, provides a more specific indication of the social costs incurred by neo-conservative and right-wing, free-market policies recently put into place:

> You [Greenspan] talk about an improving economy while we have lost 3 million private sector jobs in the last two years, long-term unemployment is more than tripled, unemployment is higher than it's been since 1994. We have a $4 billion national debt, 1.3 million Americans have lost their health insurance, millions of seniors can't afford prescription drugs, middle-class families can't send their kids to college because they don't have the money to do that, bankruptcy cases have increased by a record-breaking 23 percent, business investment is at its lowest level in more than 50 years, CEOs make more than 500 times what their workers make, the middle class is shrinking, we have the greatest gap between the rich and the poor of any industrialized nation, and this is an economy that is improving?[15]

President Bush sees no irony in proclaiming in one speech after another, largely to selected groups of conservatives, that he is a "born again" Christian, all the while passing legislation that: weakens environmental laws such as the Clean Air Act; opposes a United Nations resolution to fund global AIDS education and prevention; undermines the stability of Medicare; wages a budget war against disadvantaged children; denies millions of poor working adults a child tax credit; squanders the federal surplus on tax cuts for the rich; and increases corporate welfare to the tune of $125 billion, just as he decreases social benefits for millions of Americans, especially those who are poverty-stricken, old, young, and disabled.[16]

Religious fundamentalism appears to be growing in the United

States and the movement has received an enormous boost from those in power who think of themselves as "chosen." At the same time, this mounting religious fervour, with its Manichean division of the world into the modalities of good and evil, remains inhospitable to dissent and reinforces a distinctly undemocratic view of patriotism. The slide into self-righteousness and intolerance appears to be on the rise in American life as politicians and moralists lay claim to an alleged monopoly on the truth, based on their religious convictions—an outlandish presumption matched only by disdain for those who do not share their worldview.[17] Under the Bush administration patriotism is now legitimated through a physics of power not held accountable and unquestioned authority, defined crudely in the dictum, "Either you are with us or with the terrorists."[18] When millions all over the world protested the US invasion of Iraq, not to mention the protests of numerous international allies, Bush and his evangelical counsellors dismissed such criticism as evidence of weakness and a refusal to acknowledge evil. As Gary Wills sums up: "Question the policy, and you no longer believe in evil—which is the same, in this context, as not believing in God. That is the religious test on which our president is grading us."[19]

This culture of intolerance and patriotic jingoism is shared and legitimated by the corporate-controlled media and an army of intellectual cheerleaders, largely bankrolled by a powerful, conservative money-machine, including the Olin, Heritage, Coors, and Scaife Family foundations. Such absolutes, of course, have little respect for difference, dissent, or even democracy itself. Politics, in this instance, has much less in common with public engagement, dialogue, and democratic governance than with a heavy reliance on institutions that rule through fear and, if necessary, brute force. Right-wing media favourite Ann Coulter asserts in her book *Treason* that "liberals are either traitors or idiots,"[20] and argues elsewhere as well that John Walker, the young American captured in Afghanistan, should be given the death penalty "in order to physically intimidate liberals, by making them realize that they can be killed too. Otherwise they can be turned into outright traitors."[21] Kathleen Parker, a conservative columnist, published an article in which she cites, without challenging, a quote from "a friend" who suggested that a number of Democratic Party candidates "should be lined up and shot."[22] And further, on the syndicated radio talk show, *Savage Nation*, aired on May 10 and 11, 2004, conservative host Michael Savage referred to Abu Ghraib prison as "Grab-an-Arab prison" and stated, "We need more of the humiliation, not less.... there should be no mercy shown to the sub-humans. I believe that a thousand of them should be killed tomorrow. I think a thousand of them held in the Iraqi prison should be [put on] trail and executed.... They should put dynamite in their behinds and drop them from thirty-five thousand feet, the whole pack of scum out of that jail."[23] In addition, James Dobson, founder of the powerful right-wing Christian organization Focus on the Family and noted evangelical leader, has compared proponents of gay marriage to Nazis and supported political candidates who have advocated executing abortion providers.

Rhetorical excesses aside, conservatives at the highest levels of government are now passing legislation to eliminate tenure, label dissent as unpatriotic, and force universities—through spurious appeals to ideological balance—to hire academics on the basis of their ideological beliefs. Right-wingers such as Lynne Cheney, conservative Christian organizations such as the American Family Association, and conservative politicians have launched an insidious attack on post-colonial theory, Middle Eastern Studies, critical pedagogy, and any field "which generates critical inquiry and thought often in opposition to the aims of the U.S. State" and the Bush regime.[24] This is the same group who believes that gay married couples occupy the same status as terrorists, while saying nothing about US involvement in the torture and abuse at Abu Ghraib prison, or the US policy of Extraordinary Rendition that allows the CIA to kidnap people and send them to authoritarian countries, such as Syria and Egypt, to be tortured.

The nature of the attack on higher education can be seen in the attempts by conservative legislators in Ohio and a number of other states to pass bills such as the Academic Bill of Rights, which argues that academics should be hired on the basis of their conservative ideology in order to balance out faculties dominated by left-wing professors and to control what conservative students are taught, allegedly immunizing them against ideas that might challenge or offend their ideological comfort zones. It gets worse. The governor of Colorado has recently called for the firing of Ward Churchill because of an essay he wrote shortly after 9/11 condemning US foreign policy; and a US congressman from New York, Anthony Weiner, has called for the firing of Joseph Massad, a Columbia University professor who has been critical of Israeli policies against Palestinians. Under the guise of patriotic correctness, conservatives want to fire prominent academics such as Churchill and Massad because of their opposition to US foreign policy, completely ignoring the quality of their intellectual scholarship. Challenging the current conservative wisdom—that is, holding views at odds with conservative orthodoxy—has now become the grounds for being labelled as un-American or being dismissed from one's job. For instance, David Horowitz, a favourite benefactor of the conservative Olin Foundation, has insisted that the "250 peace studies programs in America teach students to identify with America's terrorist enemies and to identify America as a Great Satan."[25] Sacrificed in this assault on higher education are the notions that a vibrant democracy cannot exist without educated citizens and that, for a "robust democracy we need more than rational deliberation, we need public realms that remind us that [democratically informed] politics matter."[26] Clearly, more is at stake here than the absence of public intellectuals to theorize and teach about the promise of a radical and inclusive democracy. The real crisis is the devaluation of the university as a democratic public sphere and the downgrading of the importance of critical education to democracy itself.

Such rhetorical and legislative interventions are about more than eliminating the critical function of dissent or of thinking itself—both vital to the democratic health of a society; they embody a kind of symbolic violence reminiscent of a totalitarian ideology, in which the suggestion that critics should be targeted and punished became a gruesome reality. Put differently, the embrace of anti-intellectualism and distrust of critical thought and oppositional intellectuals support authoritarianism over and against democracy. Such rhetoric cannot be dismissed as an aberration. Unfortunately, this kind of extreme language is not only found among eccentric right-wing intellectuals; it is also on prominent display in mainstream Republican Party rhetoric. For example, when the Republican Party launched its 2004 campaign to re-elect George W. Bush, it produced an ad that stated, "Some are now attacking the president for attacking the terrorists." As rhetorically dishonest as it is opportunistic, the ad misrepresents the complexity of a post-9/11 world and suggests that critics of Bush's policies support terrorism. Critics are not supporting terrorism. Instead, they are pointing out that the Bush administration has squandered much-needed funds by invading Iraq and, in doing so, has lost sight of the real threats posed by terrorists, while seriously "undermining the campaign against terrorism."[27]

I am not suggesting that all conservatives support this kind of sophistry or believe in these deeply undemocratic sentiments and actions, though I am concerned by the refusal of many prominent conservatives to condemn the McCarthyite, if not fascistic, ranting of the likes of Ann Coulter, Rush Limbaugh, Pat Robertson, James Dobson, and Michael Savage, among others. I do think the right-wing takeover of the Republican Party, especially with the re-election of Bush in 2004, and its relentless appeal to the moral high ground—coupled with its ongoing demonization and punishment of those on the Right and Left who dare to question its policies—shut down the possibility for dialogue and exchange, thereby silencing those who wish to make power visible, as well as politically and morally accountable, in a democracy. But this type of politics does more than celebrate its own intolerance; it also lays the groundwork for a kind of authoritarianism that views democracy as both a burden and a threat.

As the federal government is restructured under the Bush administration, it relies more heavily on its militarizing functions, giving free rein to the principle of security at the expense of public service, and endorsing property rights over human rights. As a consequence, democracy is imperilled as the emerging security state offers the American people the false choice between being safe or being free.[28] In the name of security, the distinction between government authority and constitutional "laws governing the rights of people accused of a crime"[29] is lost. A web of secrecy has emerged under the Bush administration that gives it the opportunity to abuse democratic freedoms and, at the same time, make itself unaccountable for its actions by using national security to its legal advantage. Under the veil of legislated secrecy, the United States government can now name individuals as terrorists without offering them a public hearing, and break into private homes and tap the phones of US citizens without a warrant. As if this were not bad enough, constitutional freedoms and civil liberties are further compromised by the power of government agents to subpoena anybody's telephone, medical, bookstore, library or university records "simply by certifying that the records are needed for an investigation of international terrorism."[30] The CIA and Pentagon are allowed to engage in domestic intelligence work, and the USA PATRIOT Act allows people to be detained secretly and indefinitely without access to lawyers or a jury trial.[31] Even children as young as fourteen years old have been held without legal representation as "enemy combatants" in possibly inhumane conditions at the military's infamous Camp Delta at Guantanamo Bay, Cuba, along with more than five hundred others who are still being detained. Most recently, it has been revealed that the US government, under a CIA program called "Extraordinary Rendition," can kidnap suspected terrorists, hold them without charges or due process of law, and send them to foreign countries known for torturing people.[32] In one highly publicized incident, Mahar Arar, a Syrian-born Canadian citizen was sent to Syria and tortured after being abducted at JFK airport by the CIA. Arar claims he was subjected to beatings and held under brutal conditions for a year. He was finally released without being charged with any crime. It has been estimated that since the September 11th attacks, "the CIA has flown 100 to 150 suspected terrorists from one foreign country to another, including to Egypt, Syria, Saudi Arabia, Jordan and Pakistan."[33] Under such circumstances, as Arundhati Roy argues, "the fundamental governing principles of democracy are not just being subverted but deliberately sabotaged. This kind of democracy is the problem, not the solution."[34] Dissent — a fundamental condition of a vibrant democracy — does not come easy in a country where people can be detained, deported, tried without representation, and held indefinitely in a jail under a legal policy of enforced secrecy.

Authoritarianism's shadow becomes increasingly darker as society is organized around a culture of unquestioned obedience, fear, cynicism, and self interest—a society in which the government promotes legislation urging neighbours to spy on each other, and the President endorses a notion of patriotism based on moral absolutes and an alleged Christian mandate to govern.[35] The arrogance of power is on full display as both the President and the Attorney General, in the name of national security, have refused to give congressional committees information they have requested about a range of government actions, including Vice-President Cheney's meetings in the White House with representatives of the energy industry and materials related to the government's anti-terrorist policies prior to the tragic events of 9/11. The Bush administration's obsession with secrecy was shamelessly invoked when the President and Vice-President agreed to appear before the 9/11 Commission only if the meeting took place behind closed doors; they did not have to testify under oath; and the session would not be recorded. With the re-election of the Bush-Cheney cabal, the arrogance of power seems to have ascended into a higher stratosphere as religious extremists, neo-conservatives, and free-market fundamentalists intensify the war in Iraq, mull over a possible attack on Iran, and prepare to privatize social security while increasing their attempt to dismantle the welfare state and to use government power to allow capital and finance to run amok in pursuing profits and power.

The New Rhetoric of Proto-Fascism

It is against the restructuring of American power and ideology that a number of critics at home and across the globe have begun to suggest that a new form of political tyranny is emerging in the United States that threatens not only its underlying democratic values, but also peace abroad.[36] The chorus of complaints and criticisms is disturbing. One of the world's most respected elder statesmen, South African leader Nelson Mandela, claimed in an interview with *Newsweek* that George W. Bush's rhetoric about democracy is a sham, and that US foreign policy is motivated by a "desire to please the arms and oil industries in the United States." He further argued that a foreign policy built on the unilateral right to invade alleged enemies undermines the United Nations and sets a dangerous standard in foreign affairs for the enemies of democracy. In light of the United States invasion of Iraq, Mandela insisted, "the United States has become a threat to world peace."[37] He is not alone in thinking this. In a survey of 7500 Europeans, the United States was ranked second, above even Kim Jong Il's nuclear-armed North Korea and terrorist-sponsoring Iran, as the greatest threat to world peace.[38] Ken Livingston, the mayor of London, denounced George W. Bush as "the greatest threat to life on this planet that we've most probably ever seen."[39]

An equally disturbing critique has emerged, suggesting that the United States government not only poses a danger to world peace, but has abdicated its democratic traditions—and its "conserving" values—in favour of radical extremism. As George Soros, respected philanthropist and multi-billionaire, puts it: "The Republican Party has been captured by a bunch of extremists."[40] Senator Robert Byrd, on the floor of Congress in

AGAINST THE NEW AUTHORITARIANISM

October 2003, went so far as to compare Bush's use of the media to the propaganda techniques employed by the leaders of the Third Reich. Drawing comparisons between the Bush administration and the infamous Nazi murderer, Herman Goering, Byrd offered a biting criticism of the growing extremism in the Bush administration.[41] In his book *Made in Texas*, Michael Lind argues that Bush is one of the worst presidents in American history and that his mission is to carry out the economic and foreign policy agenda of the far Right.[42] The notion of extremism has also been raised by former national security advisor to President Jimmy Carter, Zbigniew Brzezinski, who claims that the Bush administration's "war on terrorism" represents "a rather narrow and extremist vision of foreign policy of the world's primary superpower."[43] Administration insiders such as Karen Kwiatowski, a former Air Force lieutenant and specialist in the office of the Undersecretary of Defense for Policy, claims that "the country has been hijacked" by neo-conservatives who are running a shadow government.[44] And, in response to Bush's radical market fundamentalism and neo-liberal ideology—with its belief that the market should be the organizing principle for all political, social, and economic decisions—American Nobel Prize laureate for economics, George A. Akerlof, stated in an interview with *Der Spiegel* magazine that

> this is the worst government the US has ever had in its more than 200 years of history. It has engaged in extraordinarily irresponsible policies not only in foreign and economic but also in social and environmental policy. This is not normal government policy. Now is the time for people to engage in civil disobedience.[45]

16

BETRAYING DEMOCRACY

Pulitzer prize-winning investigative journalist Seymour Hersh has argued that the United States government "has been taken over basically by a cult, eight or nine neo-conservatives have somehow grabbed the government. ... You have to wonder what a Democracy is when it comes down to a few men in the Pentagon and a few men in the White House having their way."[46] In his most recent book, *Crimes against Nature*, Robert F. Kennedy, Jr. implies that the United States marks the triumph of corporate power over democracy and, as a consequence, has become a fascist country. Quoting Franklin Roosevelt, Kennedy writes, "the liberty of a democracy is not safe if the people tolerate the growth of private power to a point where it becomes stronger than their democratic state itself. That, in its essence, is fascism."[47] An even more serious and sustained attack against the Bush administration has emerged among a number of critics who claim that the United States is increasingly abandoning democracy altogether, as it descends into the icy political waters of a new form of authoritarianism.

More recently, Chris Hedges, writing in *Harper's*, has suggested that the Christian Right's aim "to transform the United States into a global Christian empire "poses the threat of a different kind of fascism from what was evident in Nazi Germany. He claims that "fascism ... would not return wearing swastikas and brown shirts. Its ideological inheritors would cloak themselves in the language of the bible; they would come carrying crosses and chanting the Pledge of Allegiance."[48]

Two critics who have received attention in the popular press for such arguments are Arundhati Roy, Indian novelist and social activist, and

AGAINST THE NEW AUTHORITARIANISM

Sheldon Wolin, emeritus professor of politics at Princeton University. Both individuals have argued that the spectre of a creeping fascism is becoming a reality in the United States and that democracy is not just being challenged but transformed by an authoritarianism that, almost unnoticed, is shaping political culture and daily life. According to Roy, the commanding institutions of American life have now been sold to the highest bidder, largely subverted by neo-liberal capitalists who have "mastered the technique of infiltrating the instruments of democracy—the 'independent' judiciary, the 'free' press ... and molding them to their purpose."[49] Roy is particularly concerned about the corporate control of the media in the United States and the role it plays in perpetuating an ultra-patriotic fervour that shuts down dissent and leaves dominant power free from responsibility for its actions. She points in particular to Clear Channel Communications, the largest radio broadcaster in the United States, reaching over 200 million people. It has organized pro-war rallies, refused to play artists critical of the war, and engaged in ongoing efforts not only to manufacture consent, but also the news itself.[50] Citing how democracy is undermined by the commercialization of public space, the control of the media, the ongoing erosion of civil liberties, the rise of repressive state power, and the emergence of an era of systemic automated surveillance—all of which is reinforced by the alleged war against terrorism—Roy argues that the price of alleged new democracy in Iraq and other countries is the "death of real democracy at home."[51] In light of these dramatic shifts away from democratic principles and social relations, she asserts that American society has entered an historical period when dominant economic and state power have removed themselves from the dynamics of political constraint and public accountability. The overall result is that the space of freedom is undermined, constituting a step towards fascism. She writes:

> The incipient, creeping fascism of the past few years has been groomed by many of our "democratic" institutions. Everyone has flirted with it—[Congress], the press, the police, the administration, the public. Even "secularists" have been guilty of helping to create the right climate. Each time you defend the right of an institution, any institution (including the Supreme Court), to exercise unfettered, unaccountable power that must never be challenged, you move toward fascism. To be fair, perhaps not everyone recognized the early signs for what they were.[52]

Roy was heavily criticized in the American media for opposing the war in Iraq, the implication being that such criticism amounted to supporting terrorism. This position was legitimated in the highest reaches of the government and stated publicly by former Attorney General John Ashcroft[53]—a charge I've already established as routine. Roy was also roundly condemned for suggesting that the United States was increasingly behaving like a fascist state.[54] Roy's use of the term "fascism" was intended not so much to imply a crude parallel between the Bush administration and Hitler's Nazi Germany, as it was to suggest how extremist the Republican Party has become since the appointment of George W. Bush in 2000.

Sheldon Wolin, a world-renowned political theorist, wrote a much more damning article about the growing authoritarianism in the United

States. Refusing to engage in rhetorical excesses, Wolin argues that "we are facing forms of domination that exceed the old vocabulary and so we have to try to find language that corresponds to this condition."[55] Rather than argue that the United States has become an authoritarian regime in the manner of Nazi Germany or fascist Italy during the 1930s and 1940s, Wolin, like Roy, argues that the United States exhibits both similarities to and differences from these regimes. Specifically, the United States shares with both these totalitarian societies an administration and political party whose aim is "to promote empire abroad and corporate [interests] at home," while at the same time "seeking total power."[56] Wolin argues that the Bush administration is moving towards an "inverted totalitarianism," and that in sharing the Nazi "aspiration toward unlimited power and aggressive expansionism, their methods and actions seem upside down."[57] Whereas the Nazis filled the streets with thugs in their drive towards unlimited power, the Bush administration centres its power in the unbridled reach of government and the massively concentrated power of a corporate-controlled media. While the Nazis subordinated big business to the political regime, under the Bush regime, corporate power shapes political policy. In addition, "While Nazi totalitarianism strove to give the masses a sense of collective power and strength, *Kraft durch Freude* ("Strength Through Joy"), inverted totalitarianism promotes a sense of weakness, of collective futility."[58] For Wolin, these differences suggest a departure in the way political power is mobilized and a reconfiguration of the institutional and social agents at the heart of such a struggle. But, in both cases, the aim is the same: the elimination of democracy, and the concentration of power and control in the hands of a single party and the ruling corporate elite. According to Wolin, all the elements are in place for what he calls the "attempted transformation of a tolerably free society into a variant of the extreme regimes of the past century." He writes:

> Thus the elements are in place: a weak legislative body, a legal system that is both compliant and repressive, a party system in which one party, whether in opposition or in the minority, is bent upon reconstituting the existing system so as to permanently favor a ruling class of the wealthy, the well-connected and the corporate, while leaving the poorer citizens with a sense of helplessness and political despair, and, at the same time, keeping the middle classes dangling between fear of unemployment and expectations of fantastic rewards once the new economy recovers. That scheme is abetted by a sycophantic and increasingly concentrated media; by the integration of universities with their corporate benefactors; by a propaganda machine institutionalized in well-funded think tanks and conservative foundations; by the increasingly closer cooperation between local police and national law enforcement agencies aimed at identifying terrorists, suspicious aliens and domestic dissidents.[59]

This book is an attempt to take critics such as Kennedy Jr., Roy, and Wolin seriously and to argue that a number of anti-democratic tendencies now threaten American democracy. Hannah Arendt recognized the essence of totalitarianism in a form of terrorism through which governments eliminated the capacity of people to engage in critical speech and autonomous action.[60] Under such circumstances, the state increasingly rules within a state of emergency justified through an alleged all-out attack on terrorism,[61] laws are suspended, democracy is slowly liquidated, and the brute power of authoritarianism descends over every aspect of public life. This descent into authoritarianism represents a combination of old and new fascist tendencies, and demands new vocabularies of resistance, a new understanding of politics and power, and a willingness to make the fight for democracy central to what it means to theorize a viable politics for the twenty-first century.

I take up some of these issues in this book. More specifically, I argue in Chapter One that the United States is on the road to a new form of authoritarianism, which can be recognized in the rise of a ruthless market fundamentalism, the emergence of a form of religious and patriotic correctness that substitutes blind faith for critical reason, the growing militarization of everyday life, a regime of surveillance and fear, the corporate control of all elements of the dominant media, and an educational fundamentalism aimed at destroying critical education as a foundation for an engaged citizenry and a vibrant democracy. In the second chapter, I examine the tragic events of Abu Ghraib and analyze the conditions that made such an event possible, all the while trying to understand the role that education plays in creating violations of human rights that one largely attributes to authoritarian regimes. In the third chapter, I focus more on the need for progressives to develop a language of hope as a condition for critically engaged politics and the emergence of new social formations. Finally, I end this short book with an interview that locates my own politics in the sense of moral outrage and a move to Canada prompted, in part, by the political and economic repression against minorities of race, colour, and sexual orientation that registered a new turn in the United States since the 1980s and emerged in full force with the re-election of George W. Bush in 2004.

1   Sheldon S. Wolin, "A Kind of Fascism is Replacing Our Democracy," Long Island NY *Newsday*, July 18, 2003. Available online: www.commondreams.org/views03/0718-07.htm.

2   Walter Cronkite, "The Trial of Saddam Hussein," *DenverPost.com*, December 21, 2003. Available on-line: www.denverpost.com/Stories0,141336-1839593,00.html. An extensive list of international agreements broken by the United States can be found in Rich Du Boff, "Mirror Mirror on the Wall, Who's the Biggest Rogue of All?," *ZNet Commentary*, August 7, 2003. Available online: www.znet.org.

3   Noam Chomsky, "There is Good Reason to Fear Us," *Toronto Star*, September 7, 2003. Available on-line: www.commondreams.org/views03/0907-03.htm.

4   Byrd, "Challenging 'Pre-emption.'"

5   This policy is spelled out in great detail in Donald Kagan, Gary Schmitt, and Thomas Donnelly (principal author), *Rebuilding America's Defenses* (Washington, DC: A Report of the Project for the New American Century, September 2000).

6   See Christopher Scheer, Lakshmi Chaudhry, and Robert Scheer David, *The Five Biggest Lies Bush Told Us about Iraq* (New York: Seven Stories Press, 2003); David Corn, *The Lies of George W. Bush* (New York: Crown Publishers, 2003). The most damning evidence that the Bush administration lied about going to war in Iraq can be found in the Downing Street Memo. The memo revealed that Bush was determined to go to war with Iraq in the summer of 2002 and had US intelligence "fix" the data to support claims about the presence of WMD. See Mark Danner, "Secret Way to War," *New York Review of Books*, 52, no. 10 (June 9, 2005). On-line: www.nybooks.com/contents/20050526.

7   Mark Trevelyn, "Bush Challenged on 'Safer America' Union Message," *Reuters*, January 21, 2004. Available on-line: www.commondreams.org/cgi-bin/print.cgi?file=headlines04/0121-04.htm.

8   Robert Jay Lifton, "American Apocalypse," *The Nation* (December 22, 2003), 12. These themes are developed extensively in Robert Jay Lifton, *Super Power Syndrome: America's Apocalyptic Confrontation with the World* (New York: Thunder Mouth Press, 2003).

9   Joel Havemann, "$1.3 Trillion in Deficits Forecast over Decade," *Los Angeles Times*, January 25, 2005. Available on-line: http://www.latimes.com/news/nationworld/nation/la-012505budget_lat,0,1493879.story?coll=la-home-headlines. For an extensive

analysis of the budget deficit, see Richard Kagan, "Deficit Picture Even Grimmer than New CBO Projections Suggest," Center on Budget and Policy Priorities (August 26, 2003). Available on-line: http://www.cbpp.org/8-26-03bud.htm.

10 On the tax issue, see Paul Krugman, *Fuzzy Math: The Essential Guide to the Bush Tax Plan* (New York: Norton, 2001).

11 Larry Wheeler and Robert Benincase, "State Budget Belt-Tightening Squeezes Health Care for Kids," *USA Today*, Friday, December 19, 2003, 15A.

12 Center on Budget and Policy Priorities, "Up to 1.6 Million Low-Income People—Including About Half a Million Children—Are Losing Health Coverage Due to State Budget Cuts" (December 22, 2003). Available on-line: http://www.cbpp.org/12-22-03health-pr.htm.

13 Paul Krugman, "Bush's Class-War Budget," *The New York Times*, February 11, 2005, A23.

14 Ibid.

15 Common Dreams News Center, "Rep Bernie Sanders vs. Chairman Alan Greenspan," *Common Dreams News Center* (July 16, 2003). Available on-line: www.commondreams.org/views03/0716-13.htm.

16 Cited in Bernie Sanders, "USA: Ex-Im Bank, Corporate Welfare at its Worst," *Corporate Watch* (May 15, 2002):1. Available on-line: www.corpwatch.org/news/PND.jsp?articleid=2570.

17 Jackson Lears, "How a War Became a Crusade," *The New York Times,* March 11, 2003, A29.

18 President George W. Bush, "September 11, 2001, Terrorist Attacks on the United States." Address to Joint Session of Congress.

19 Gary Wills, "With God on His Side," *The New York Times Sunday Magazine* (March 30, 2003): 29.

20 Ann Coulter, *Treason: Liberal Treachery from the Cold War to the War on Terrorism* (New York: Crown Forum, 2003): 16.

21 Cited in Jay Bookman, "Ann Coulter Wants to Execute You," *The Atlanta Journal-Constitution*, February 18, 2002. Available on-line: www.indybay.org/news/20002/02/116560.php.

22 Kathleen Parker, "Politics Are Out of Place in a Time of War," *Townhall*, November 1, 2003. Available on-line: www.townhall.com/columinists/Kathleenparker/

kp20031101.shtml.

23 Cited in "Savage Nation: It's Not Just Rush," *Media Matters for America*, May 13, 2004. Available on-line: http://mediamatters.org/items/200405130004.

24 A. Naomi Paik. "Education and Empire, Old and New," unpublished paper, Yale University. January 8, 2005.

25 Robert Ivie. "Academic Freedom and Political Heresy," unpublished manuscript.

26 Margaret Kohn. "The Mauling of Public Space," *Dissent* (Spring 2001): 77.

27 Paul Krugman, "The Uncivil War," *The New York Times*, November 25, 2003, A29.

28 For a brilliant analysis of the link between the Bush administration's war on terrorism and the assault on constitutional freedoms, see David Cole, *Enemy Aliens: Double Standards and Constitutional Freedoms in the War on Terrorism* (New York: The New Press, 2003).

29 Ben Bagdikian, "Beware the Geeks Bearing Lists," *ZNet Commentary* (December 24, 2002). Available on-line: www.Zmag.org/sustainers.content/2002-12/07bagdikian. cfm.

30 Anthony Lewis, "Un-American Activities," *New York Review of Books* 16 (October 23, 2003), 18.

31 This issue is taken up in great detail in Cynthia Brown, ed., *Lost Liberties: Ashcroft and the Assault on Personal Freedom* (New York: The New Press, 2003); Nat Hentoff, *The War on the Bill of Rights and the Gathering Resistance* (New York: Seven Stories Press, 2003); and David Cole, *Enemy Aliens* (New York: The New Press, 2003).

32 The best article on this subject is Jane Mayer, "Outsourcing Torture," *The New Yorker* (February 14, 2005), 106-123.

33 Douglas Jehl and David Johnston, "Rule Change Lets C.I.A. Freely Send Suspects Abroad to Jails," *The New York Times*, March 6, 2005, 1.

34 Arundhati Roy, *War Talk* (Boston: South End Press, 2003) 34.

35 Juan Stam, "Bush's Religious Language," *The Nation* (December 22, 2003): 27.

36 There are many excellent books dealing with the rise of right-wing authoritarianism in the United States. Some examples include: Charles Higham, *American Swastika* (New York: Doubleday, 1985); Susan Canedy, *America's Nazis* (Menlo Park: Markgraf Publications, 1990); Russ Bellant, *Old Nazis, The New Right, and the Republican Party* (Boston: South End Press, 1991); Paul Hainsworth, ed., *The Extreme Right in Europe and North America* (London: Pinter, 1992); Chip Berlet, Matthew Lyons, and Su-

zanne Phar, eds., *Eyes Right: Challenging the Right-Wing Backlash* (Boston: South End Press, 1995); Sara Diamond, *Roads to Domination: Right-Wing Movements and Political Power in the United States* (New York: Guilford Press, 1995); Michael Novick, *White Lies, White Power* (Monroe: Common Courage Press, 1995); Lyman Tower Sargent, ed., *Extremism in America* (New York: New York University Press, 1995); Chip Berlet and Matthew Lyons, *Right-Wing Populism in America: Too Close for Comfort* (New York: Guilford Press, 2000); Martin A. Lee, *The Beast Reawakens: Fascism's Resurgence from Hitler's Sypmasters to Today's Neo-Nazi Groups and Right-Wing Extremists* (New York: Routledge, 2000).

37 *Newsweek* Interview, "Nelson Mandela: The U.S.A. Is a Threat to World Peace," *Newsweek* Web Exclusive (September 11, 2002). Available on-line: www.msnbc.com/news/806174.asp?cp1=1.

38 "European Majority Sees United States as Greatest Threat to World Security, Above Even North Korea," *Newsweek* Web Exclusive (November 7, 2003). Available on-line: www.intelmessages.org/messsages/National_Security/wwwboard/messages_03/6148.

39 Nigel Morris, "Livingston Says Bush is 'Greatest Threat to Life on Planet,'" *The Independent/UK* (November 18, 2003). Available on-line: http://portland.indymedia.org/en/2003/11/275040.shtml.

40 See "George Soros Interview on NOW with Bill Moyers," (September 12, 2003). Transcript available on-line: http://www.pbs.org/now/. Soros develops this position in greater detail in George Soros, *The Bubble of American Supremacy* (New York: Public Affairs, 2004).

41 This issue is discussed in Harvey Wasserman and Bob Fitrakis, "Senator Byrd, Major Media Spread Coverage of Bush-Nazi Nexus," *Columbus Free Press*, (October 22, 2003). Available on-line: http://www.scoop.co.nz/mason/stories/HL0310/S00193.htm. On the same day this story broke, the Associated Press ran a national story connecting President Bush's grandfather, Prescott Bush, to Adolf Hitler. Bush's grandfather, it appears, had his bank seized by the federal government because he had helped finance Adolf Hitler's rise to power.

42 Michael Lind, *Made in Texas: George W. Bush and the Southern Takeover of American Politics* (New York: Basic Books, 2002).

43 Zbiginiew Brzezinski, "To Lead, US Must Give up Paranoid Policies," *The Interna-*

27

tional Herald Tribune (November 15, 2003). Available on-line: www.commondreams. org/headlines03/1115-01.htm.

44 Rift Goldstein, "Cheney's Hawks 'Hijacking Policy,'" *Common Dreams* (October 30, 2003). Available on-line: http://www.commondreams.org/headlines03/1030-08.htm.

45 Matthias Streitz, "US Nobel Laureate Slams Bush Gov't as 'Worst' in American History," *Der Spiegel* (July 29, 2003). Available on-line: www.commondreams.org/headlines03/0729-06.htm.

46 Seymour Hersh, "We've Been Taken Over by a Cult," *Democracy Now* (January 26, 2005). Available online: http://www.democracynow.org/article.pl?sid=05/01/26/1450204.

47 Robert F. Kennedy, Jr., *Crimes against Nature* (New York: Harper Collins, 2005), 193.

48 Chris Hedges, "Feeling the Hate with the National Religious Broadcasters," *Harper's* (May 2005), p.61.

49 Arundhati Roy, "Instant-Mix Imperial Democracy (Buy One, Get One Free)," *Common Dreams* (May 18, 2003). Available on-line: http://www.commondreams.org/views03/0518- 01.htm.

50 Roy, "Instant-Mix Imperial Democracy."

51 Ibid.

52 Arundhati Roy, *War Talk* (Cambridge: South End Press, 2003), pp. 36-37. On the growing right-wing politicization of the United States Supreme Court, see Martin Garbus, *Courting Disaster: The Supreme Court and the Unmaking of American Law* (New York: Times Book, 2002).

53 See "Testimony of Attorney General John Ashcroft to the Senate Committee on the Judiciary" (December 6, 2001). Available on-line: www.usdoj.gov/ag/testimony/2001/.

54 Roy has been lambasted in the conservative *Weekly Standard*, which gave her the facetious "Susan Sontag Award" for anti-war comments. *The New Republic* followed suit with its equally absurd "Idiocy Award." Roy responded to the increasing chorus of criticism with an article in *The Guardian*, in which she argued that the label of Anti-Americanism she was charged with simply meant that "the chances are that he or she will be judged before they're heard and the argument will be lost in the welter of bruised national pride." See Arundhati Roy, "Not Again," *The Guardian* (September 27, 2002). Available on-line: www.ratical.org/ratville/CAH/AR092702.html.

55 Wolin cited in Alexander Stile, "The Latest Obscenity Has Seven Letters," *The New York Times*, September 13, 2003, B17.
56 Sheldon Wolin, "Inverted Totalitarianism: How the Bush Regime Is Effecting the Transformation to a Fascist-Like State," *The Nation* (May 19, 2003), 13.
57 Ibid., 13-14.
58 Ibid.
59 Ibid., 14.
60 Hannah Arendt, *The Origins of Totalitarianism* (New York: Allen and Unwin, 1967).
61 This theme is taken up brilliantly in Giorgio Agamben, *State of Exception* (Chicago: University of Chicago Press, 2005).

1

AMERICA'S TURN TOWARD AUTHORITARIANISM

The re-election of George W. Bush makes clear what most dominant intellectuals on the left and right have refused to acknowledge. The United States is not simply a centre-right government supported by the majority of the populace; it is a country moving rapidly towards a form of authoritarianism that undermines any claim to a practicing liberal democracy. For those who cling to the illusion of democracy, even in its damaged forms, the issues that appear the most injurious to democracy will be the war in Iraq, the record trade deficit, a soaring budget deficit, a weak economy, the Bush-Cheney assault on civil liberties, the rise of unbridled militarism, and the growing concentration of wealth in the hands of the rich and elite corporations. Although seen as posing a threat to democracy, these issues are generally viewed as not being comparable to the US government's establishing the foundation for a new, emerging authoritarianism. For instance, oppositional critics such as George Monbiot believe that the Bush project is less about the rise of "soft fascism" than the emergence of puritanism as a justifying, religious ideology used to legitimate the "enrichment of the elite and the impoverishment of the lower classes."[1] Liberal apologists such as James Traub, a feature writer for the *New York Times*, put a different spin on the authoritarian direction in which the United States is moving. For Traub, any comparison between the Bush administration and fascism "constitutes a gross trivialization of the worst event in modern history."[2] According to Traub, fascism is a term that was abused by the Left in the 1960s and is being used recklessly once again by those criticizing the Bush regime. His argument suggests that fascism is an historically specific movement whose ideology cannot be applied outside the conditions from which it emerged. In short, Traub implies that any suggestion that the United States is becoming a fascist state is preposterous. Traub, like Monbiot, believes that whatever problems the United States faces have nothing to do with a growing authoritarianism. On the contrary, according to this view, we are simply witnessing the seizure of power by some extremists who not only represent a form of political exceptionalism, an annoying growth on the body politic, but also have little to do with the real values that constitute the meaning of American democracy and national identity. At ease with the increasing repressions established under the Bush administration as well as with the violations of civil liberties put into place by former Attorney General John Ashcroft, Traub cites Norman Siegel, the former head of the New York Civil Liberties Union, to suggest that the USA PATRIOT Act is not related to a creeping fascism and may be well justified as part of the current war on terrorism. If Traub is to be believed, democracy in the United States is as strong as ever. However, Traub's argument is informed by the mistaken notion that the collapse of fascist regimes after World War II represented the demise of fascism. What Traub ignores is the distinction between the state-sponsored regime and fascist ideology and movements. No critic is saying that the United States now mimics the fascism of the 1930s; rather, the point is that it appears to be developing characteristics endemic to fascist ideology. Traub, in particular, like most members of the dominant media in the United States, has no sense of different degrees or gradations of authoritarianism, of fascism as an ideology that can always reconstitute itself in different ideas, practices, and arguments. Instead, he clings to both a reductive understanding of fascism and a simplistic binary logic that holds that a country is either authoritarian or democratic. He has no language for entertaining either a mixture of both systems or a degree of unaccountable power that might suggest a more updated, if not different, form of authoritarianism.

Emerging Elements of Authoritarianism and Proto-Fascism in the United States

Fascism and authoritarianism are important categories that must be mined to explore the changing nature of power, control, and rule in the United States and the challenge that such changes pose to a democracy clearly under siege. I am not suggesting the US is engaged in a process of genocidal terror against racialized populations (though the increase in police brutality in the last decade against people of colour, coupled with the rise of a prison-industrial-military complex that primarily punishes black and brown men, cannot be overlooked).[3] Nor can the increased attack by the American government on the rights of many innocent Arabs, Muslims, and immigrants be understood as anything other than a kind of totalitarian time warp in which airport terminals now resemble state prisons as foreign nationals are fingerprinted, photographed, and interrogated.[4] Rather, I am arguing that the US has many earmarks of a growing authoritarianism. Fascism is not an ideological apparatus frozen in a particular historical period, but a theoretical and political signpost pointing to how democracy can be subverted, if not destroyed. In the 1980s Bertram Gross wrote a book titled *Friendly Fascism* in which he argued that if fascism came to the United States, it would not embody the fascist characteristics associated with its legacies in the past.[5] There would be no Nuremberg rallies, doctrines of racial superiority, government-sanctioned book burnings, death camps, or the abrogation of the constitution. In short, fascism would not take the form of an ideological grid from the past that is simply downloaded onto another country under different historical conditions. On the contrary, he believed that fascism is an eternal danger and can become relevant under new conditions, taking on familiar forms of thought that resonate with nativist traditions, experiences, and political relations. Umberto Eco, in his discussion of "eternal fascism," argues that any updated version of fascism will not openly assume the mantle of historical fascism. Rather, new forms of authoritarianism will appropriate some of its elements. Like Gross, Eco argues that, if facism comes to America, it will be under a different guise, though no less destructive of democracy. He writes:

AGAINST THE NEW AUTHORITARIANISM

Ur-Fascism [a term meaning eternal fascism] is still around us, sometimes in plainclothes. It would be much easier for us if there appeared on the world scene somebody saying, "I want to reopen Auschwitz, I want the Blackshirts to parade again in the Italian squares." Life is not that simple. Ur-Fascism can come back under the most innocent of disguises. Our duty is to uncover it and to point our finger at any of its new instances—everyday, in every part of the world. Franklin Roosevelt's words of November 4, 1938, are worth recalling: "If American democracy ceases to move forward as a living force, seeking day and night by peaceful means to better the lot of our citizens, fascism will grow in strength in our land." Freedom and liberation are an unending task.[6]

To make a distinction between the old and new forms of fascism, I use the term *proto-fascism,* not only because it suggests a different constellation of elements and forms pointing towards its reconstitution, but also because it has "the beauty of familiarity, and rightly in many cases reveals a deliberate attempt to make fascism relevant in new conditions."[7] The point here is not to obscure the distinctiveness of the nature, force, or consequences of the old fascism, but to highlight how some of its central elements are emerging in contemporary forms. Precise accounts of the meaning of fascism abound, and I have no desire, given its shifting nature, to impose a rigid definition with universal pretensions. But most scholars agree that fascism is a mass movement that emerges out of a failed democracy, and its ideology is extremely anti-liberal, anti-democratic, and anti-socialist. It is also marked by an "elaborate ideology which covers all aspects of man's

34

existence and which contains a powerful chiliastic [messianic or religious] moment."[8] As a political philosophy, fascism exalts the nation and race—or some purified form of national identity—over the individual, supports centralized dictatorial power, demands blind obedience from the masses, and promotes a top-down revolution. As a social order, it is generally characterized by a system of terror directed against perceived enemies of the state; a monopolistic control of the mass media; an expanding prison system; a state monopoly of weapons; the existence of privileged groups and classes; control of the economy by a limited number of people; unbridled corporatism; "the appeal to emotion and myth rather than reason, the glorification of violence on behalf of a national cause; the mobilization and militarization of civil society; [and] an expansionist foreign policy intended to promote national greatness."[9]

Robert Paxton provides a working definition of fascism that points to its anti-democratic character and to those elements that link it to both the past and the present. Paxton's aim is not to provide precise definitions of fascism but to understand the conditions that enabled fascism to work and promote its development in the future. He defines it as

> a form of political behavior marked by obsessive preoccupation with community decline, humiliation or victimhood and by compensatory cults of unity, energy and purity, in which a mass-based party of committed nationalist militants, working in uneasy but effective collaboration with traditional elites, abandons democratic liberties and pursues with redemptive violence and without ethical or legal restraints goals of internal cleansing

and external expansion.[10]

The spectre of fascism resides in the lived relations of a given social order and the ways in which such relations exacerbate the material conditions of inequality, undercut a sense of individual and social agency, hijack democratic values, and promote a deep sense of hopelessness and cynicism. Proto-fascism, as both an ideology and a set of social practices, emerges within the contradictions that mark such relations, scorning the present while calling for a revolution that rescues a deeply anti-modernist past as a way to revolutionize the future. Mark Neocleous touches on the anti-modernist nature of fascist ideology in his discussion of a "reactionary modernism" that is typical of the new Right and essentially ultraconservative. He writes:

> [The New Right] pitted itself against the existing order—the post-war "consensus" regarding welfarism and the quasi corporate management of capitalism—in the light of an image of past national glory (a mythic and contradictory image, but no less powerful for that). The central elements of New Right politics—an aggressive leadership, uncompromising stance on law and order, illiberal attitude on moral questions generally and certain political questions such as race and immigration, an attack on the labor movement and a defense of private property, and a forthright nationalism—all combine in a politics of reaction: a reassertion of the principle of private property and capital accumulation as the raison d'etre of modern society, alongside an authoritarian moralism requiring excessive state power as a means of policing civil society. If there is such a thing as the New

Right distinct from "traditional" conservatism, then it lies in its being a reactionary modernism of our times.[11]

The emerging proto-fascism that threatens American democracy can best be understood by examining a number of characteristics that relate it to both an older form of fascism and a set of contemporary conditions that give it a distinctive identity. After documenting and analyzing these central, though far from exhaustive, features of proto-fascism, I want to conclude by examining how neoliberalism provides a unique set of conditions for producing and legitimating the central tendencies of proto-fascism.

The cult of traditionalism and a reactionary modernism are central features of proto-fascism and are alive and well in Bush's America. The alliance of neo-conservatives, extremist evangelical Christians, and free-market advocates on the political Right imagines a social order modelled on the presidency of William McKinley and the values of the robber barons. The McKinley presidency lasted from 1897 to 1901 and "had a consummate passion to serve corporate and imperial power."[12] This was an age when blacks, women, immigrants, and minorities of class "knew their place," big government served the exclusive interests of the corporate monopolists, commanding institutions were under the sway of narrow political interests, welfare was a private enterprise, and labour unions were kept in place by the repressive forces of the state. All these conditions are being reproduced under the leadership of an extremist element of the Republican Party that holds sway over all branches of government. William

Greider, writing in *The Nation*, comments on the cult of traditionalism and anti-modernism that characterizes this administration and its return to a past largely defined through egregious inequality,[13] corporate greed, hyper-commercialism, political corruption, and an utter disdain for economic and political democracy. According to Greider, the overall ambition of the Bush administration and his right-wing allies is,

> to roll back the twentieth century, quite literally. That is, de-fenestrate the federal government and reduce its scale and pow-ers to a level well below what it was before the New Deal's cen-tralization. With that accomplished, movement conservatives envision a restored society in which the prevailing values and power relationships resemble the America that existed around 1900, when William McKinley was President.... [Under such circumstances] governing authority and resources are dispersed from Washington, returned to local levels and also to individuals and private institutions, most notably corporations and religious organizations. The primacy of private property rights is re-estab-lished over the shared public priorities expressed in government regulation. Above all, private wealth—both enterprises and in-dividuals with higher incomes—are permanently insulated from the progressive claims of the graduated income tax.[14]

A second feature connecting the old fascism to its updated ver-sion is the ongoing corporatization of civil society and the diminishing of public space. The latter refers to the fact that corporate space is destroying democratic public spheres, eliminating those public spaces where norm-establishing communication takes place. Viewed primarily as an economic investment rather than as a central, democratic sphere for fostering the citizen-based processes of deliberation, debate, and dialogue, public space is being consistently diminished through the relentless dynamic of privatization and commercialization. The important notion that space can be used to cultivate citizenship is now transformed by a new "common sense," linked almost entirely to the production of consumers. The inevitable correlate to this logic is that providing space for democracy to grow is no longer a priority. As theorists such as Jürgen Habermas and David Harvey have argued, the space of critical citizenship cannot flourish without the reality of public space.[15] Put differently, "the space of citizenship is as important as the idea of citizenship."[16] As a political category, space is crucial to any critical understanding of how power circulates, how disciplinary practices are constructed, and how social control is organized. But, as Margaret Kohn points out in her landmark study on radical space, "spatial practices can also contribute to transformative politics."[17] Moreover, space as a political category performs invaluable theoretical work in connecting material struggles to ideas, theories to concrete practices, and political operations to the concerns of everyday life. Without public space, it becomes more difficult for individuals to imagine themselves as political agents or to understand the necessity for developing a discourse capable of defending civic institutions. Public space confirms the idea of individuals and groups having a public voice, thus drawing a distinction between civic liberty and market liberty. The demands of citizenship affirm the social as a political concept as well as an economic category; the sanctity of the town hall or public square in American life is grounded in the crucial recognition that citizenship has to be cultivated in non-commercialized spaces. Indeed, democracy itself needs public spheres where education, as a condition for civic discourses and critical citizenship, can flourish, where people can meet, and democratic identities, values, and relations have the time "to grow and flourish."[18] Zygmunt Bauman captures the historical importance of public spaces for nourishing civic discourses and engaging citizens as well as the ethical consequences of the current disappearances of non-commodified spheres. He writes:

> These meeting places … public spaces—agoras and forums in their various manifestations, places where agendas are set, private affairs are made public … were also the sites in which norms were created—so that justice could be done, and apportioned horizontally, thus re-forging the conversationalists into a community, set apart and integrated by the shared criteria of evaluation. Hence a territory stripped of public space provides little chance for norms being debated, for values to be confronted, to clash and to be negotiated. The verdicts of right and wrong, beauty and ugliness, proper and improper, useful and useless may only descend from on high, from regions never to be penetrated by any but a most inquisitive eye; the verdicts are unquestionable since no questions may be meaningfully addressed to the judges and since the judges left no address—not even an e-mail address—and no one can be sued where they reside. No room is left for the "local opinion leaders"; no room is left for the "local opinion" as such.[19]

A third feature of the emerging proto-fascism is the relationship between the construction of an ongoing culture of fear and a form of patriotic correctness designed to bolster rampant nationalism and selective popularism. Fear is mobilized through the war on terrorism and through "the sovereign pronouncement of a 'state of emergency' [which] generates a wild zone of power, barbaric and violent, operating without democratic oversight in order to combat an 'enemy' that threatens the existence of not merely and not mainly its citizens, but its sovereignty."[20] As Stanley Aronowitz points out, the national security state is now organized through "a combination of internal terrorism and the threat of external terrorism," which reinforces "its most repressive functions."[21] The threat of outside terrorism redefines the rules of war since there is no traditional state or enemy to fight. One consequence is that all citizens and non-citizens are viewed as potential terrorists and must prove their innocence through either consent or complicity with the national security state. Under such circumstances, patriotic fervour marks the line between terrorist and non-terrorist. Jingoistic patriotism is now mobilized in the highest reaches of government, in the media, and throughout society, put on perpetual display through the rhetoric of celebrities, journalists, and nightly television news anchors, and relentlessly buttressed by the never-ending waving of flags—on cars, trucks, clothes, houses, and the lapels of TV anchors—as well as through the use of mottoes, slogans, and songs. As a rhetorical ploy to silence dissent, patriotism is used to name as unpatriotic any attempt to make governmental power and authority accountable at home or to question how the appeal to nationalism is being used to legitimate the United States government's aspirations to empire-building overseas. This type of anti-liberal thinking is deeply distrustful of critical inquiry, mistakes meaningful dissent for treason, constructs politics on the moral absolutes of "us and them," and views difference and democracy as threats to consensus and national identity. Such "patriotic" fervour fuels a system of militarized control that not only repudiates the authority of international law, but also relies on a notion of preventive war to project the fantasies of unbridled American power all over the globe. Richard Falk argues that it is precisely this style of imperial control—fed by the desire for incontestable military preeminence in the world—and the use of authoritarian modes of regulation by the state at home that have given rise to what he describes as the threat of global fascism posed by the Bush administration. He writes:

> But why fascist? ... First of all, the combination of unchallengeable military preeminence with a rejection by the US Government of the restraining impact of international law and the United Nations. ... Secondly, the US government in moving against terrorism has claimed sweeping power to deal with the concealed Al Qaeda network. ... the character of the powers claimed include secret detentions, the authority to designate American citizens as "enemy combatants" without any rights, the public consideration of torture as a permissible police practice in anti-terrorist work, the scrutiny applied to those of Muslim faith, the reliance on assassination directed at terrorist suspects wherever they are found, and numerous invasions of privacy directed at ordinary people. ... The slide toward fascism at home is given tangible expression by these practices, but it is also furthered by an uncritical and chauvinistic patriotism, by

the release of periodic alarmist warnings of mega-terrorist immi-
nent attacks that fail to materialize, and by an Attorney General,
John Ashcroft, who seems to exult in the authoritarian approach
to law enforcement.[22]

A fourth feature of proto-fascism is the attempt to control the mass
media through government regulation, consolidated corporate ownership,
or sympathetic media moguls and spokespeople. The use of government
regulation is evident in the Bush-appointed FCC's attempts to pass legislation favouring media monopolies that would undermine opposition
and organize consent through a "capillary network of associations with
vast powers of social and cultural persuasion."[23] Indeed, media regulation
has promoted rather than limited the consolidation of media ownership
in the United States. But the Bush administration has done more than
allow corporations to take control of the media, it has also paid a number of politically friendly journalists to write in support of administration
policies. For instance, conservative black pundit Armstrong Williams was
paid $240,000 by the Bush administration to plug the administration's
educational policies and to interview Education Secretary Rod Paige on
his nationally syndicated television and radio shows. Mr. Williams was
also hired to "utilize his long-term working relationship with 'America's
Black Forum'—a black news program—to encourage producers periodi-
cally to address the No Child Left Behind Act."[24] Other journalists on
the take included syndicated columnists Maggie Gallagher and Michael
McManus, who "repeatedly defended President Bush's push for a $300

43

million initiative encouraging marriage as a way of strengthening families."[25] It gets worse. It appears that the Bush administration not only paid
journalists to pretend to be objective while pushing partisan policies; it
also manufactured its own video news programs in order to build support
for various policies pushed by the administration. Hiring actors who then
pretended to be news reporters, the Bush administration then sent out fake
news stories to television stations which ran them as if they were genuine.
Appearing largely as local news reports, these government-sponsored fake
news programs constitute nothing less than state-produced propaganda,
reaching millions of people "without any acknowledgment of the government's role in their production."[26] Beyond the deceit and disingenuousness
of such tactics, which are at odds with the role the media should play in a
democracy, there is the matter of this propaganda machine being paid for
with public funds. Such tactics are more than a violation of journalistic
and media integrity, they are a concerted effort to undermine the integrity
of a free press and its role in making the government accountable for their
power and actions. As Eric Alterman points out, "'two cheers for democracy,' wrote E.M. Forster, 'one because it admits variety and two because it
permits criticism.' But the aim of the Bush offensive against the press is to
do just the opposite; to insure, as far as possible, that only one voice is heard
and that no criticism is sanctioned. The press may be the battleground, but
the target is democracy itself."[27] Alterman is only partly right. Such policies
represent more than an attack on democracy, they provide the foundation
for a new form of authoritarianism.

As a powerful form of public pedagogy, the media set the agenda for what information is included or excluded; they provide the narratives for understanding the past and present; they distinguish between high and low status knowledge; they offer up modes of identity; they legitimate particular values; and they have the power to deeply influence how people define the future. The media do not merely manufacture consent; they go so far as to produce the news, and propose the knowledge, skills, and values through which citizenship is lived and democracy defined. In this process, the media has assumed a major role in providing the conditions necessary for creating knowledgeable citizens capable of participating fully in shaping and governing society by having access to a wide range of knowledge and information. At the risk of exaggerating this issue, I must stress that in the twenty-first century, the media, as well as the culture they produce, distribute, and sanction, have become the most important educational force in creating citizens and social agents capable of putting existing institutions into question and making democracy work—or doing just the opposite.

Unfortunately, the power of the media, along with the agenda they set, is now in the hands of a limited number of transnational corporations, and the number of owners is actually decreasing. Robert McChesney and John Nichols argue that "the U.S. media system is dominated by about ten transnational conglomerates including Disney, AOL TimeWarner, News Corporation, Viacom, Vivendi Universal, Sony, Liberty, Bertelsmann, AT&T Comcast, and General Electric (NBC)."[28] Before the Telecommunications Act of 1996, a single firm could own no more than twenty-eight radio stations nationally. With the passage of the law and the relaxation of restrictions, the radio industry has been in a state of upheaval as hundreds of stations have been sold. Three firms in the largest radio market now control access to more than half the listening audience. One of the firms, Clear Channel Communications, owns 1,225 stations in the United States and reaches "more than 70 percent of the American public."[29] Under proto-fascism, the marketplace of ideas has almost nothing to do with what is crucial for citizens to know in order to be active participants in shaping and sustaining a vibrant democracy. On the contrary, the media largely serve to target audiences for advertising, to pander to the anti-liberal ideologies of the political elite, to reinforce the conventional wisdom of corporate interests, and to promote cynical withdrawal by a populace adrift in a sea of celebrity scandal, mindless info-tainment, and the endless bigotry and hate broadcast on right-wing Christian radio and television talk shows, especially those faith-based shows that are part of the powerful Christian Broadcasting Network.[30] In a proto-fascist state, the media deteriorate into a combination of commercialism, propaganda, and entertainment.[31] Under such circumstances, they neither operate in the interests of the public good nor provide the pedagogical conditions necessary for producing critical citizens or defending a vibrant democracy. Instead, as McChesney and Nichols point out, concentrated media depoliticize the culture of politics, commercially carpet-bomb its citizens, and denigrate public life.[32] Rather than perform an essential public service, the media have become the primary tool for promoting a culture of consent in which citizens are misinformed and public discourse is debased. Media concentration restricts the range of views to which people have access and thereby does a disservice to democracy itself. For example, NOW with Bill Moyers did a radio survey through which they discovered that "the top-rated talk radio stations across the country ran 310 hours of conservative talk each day and only five hours of views that were not right-wing."[33]

A fifth element of proto-fascism is the rise of an Orwellian version of Newspeak in the United States, or what Umberto Eco labels as the language of "eternal fascism," whose purpose is to produce "an impoverished vocabulary, and an elementary syntax [whose consequence is] to limit the instruments for complex and critical reasoning."[34] Under the Bush administration, especially since the horrible events of September 11th, the tools of language, sound, and image are increasingly being appropriated. As the critical power of language is reduced in official discourse to the simulacra of communication, it becomes more difficult for the American public to engage in critical debates, translate private considerations into public concerns, and recognize the distortions and lies that underlie much of the current government policies. What happens to critical language under the emergence of official Newspeak can be seen in the various ways in which the Bush administration and its official supporters misrepresent by misnaming government policies, and simply engage in lying to cover up their own regressive politics and policies.[35]

Many people have pointed to Bush himself as a mangler of the English language, but this charge simply repeats the obvious while privatizing a much more important issue connecting language to power. Bush's discursive ineptness may be fodder for late-night comics, but such analyses miss the more strategic issue of how the Bush administration actually manipulates discourse. For instance, Bush describes himself as a "reformer" while he promotes policies that expand corporate welfare, give tax benefits to the rich, and "erode the financial capacity of the state to undertake any but the most minimal welfare functions."[36] He defines himself as a "compassionate conservative," but he implements policies that result in "billions of dollars in cuts … proposed for food stamp and child nutrition programs, and for health care for the poor."[37] Bush's public speeches, often mimicked in the media, are filled with what Renana Brooks has called "empty language," that is, statements so abstract as to be relatively meaningless, except to reinforce in simplistic terms an often reactionary ideological position. Brooks cites the example of Bush's comment on the complex relationship between malpractice suits and skyrocketing health care, which he reduces to "No one has ever been healed by a frivolous lawsuit."[38] While Bush's own ideological position becomes clear in this comment, the complexity of the issue is completely trivialized and removed from public discussion. Sometimes the distortions of official language are hard to miss, even among the media guards so quick to invoke patriotic correctness. One glaring example happened in an interview between Terry Gross, host of National Public Radio's *Fresh Air*, and Grover Norquist, president of Americans for Tax Reform, also considered to be the chief architect of President Bush's tax plan. The topic for discussion was the estate tax, reviled as the "death tax" by conservative elites to gain popular support for its repeal, though the majority of Americans will not be affected by this tax. Gross suggested that since the estate tax only effects a small minority of people who get over two million dollars in inheritance, the law eliminating it clearly privileges the rich, not the average American. Norquist responded by arguing that the morality behind her argument was comparable to the same type of morality that resulted in the death of millions of Jews under the Holocaust. When Gross challenged this specious analogy, Norquist argued illogically that people (read liberals) who attacked the estate tax could now be placed on the same moral plane as the Nazis who killed over six million Jews, and untold others.[39] Under this logic, any critique of a minority group, but especially the rich, can be dismissed as being comparable to the kind of discrimination waged by the perpetrators of one of the worse mass murders in human history. Of course, there is the further implication that liberal critics should also be punished for these views, just as the Nazis were punished in Nuremberg for their crimes against humanity. This is not just a matter of using a desperate logic to dismiss counter-arguments, or of silencing one's critics through distortion, but of actually demonizing those who hold the "wrong" views. Norquist's position is a contortion that fails to hide the fundamentalism that often drives this type of language.

Official Newspeak also trades in the rhetoric of fear in order to manipulate the public into a state of servile political dependency and un-questioning ideological support. Fear and its attendant use of moral panics create not only a rhetorical umbrella to promote other agendas, but also a sense of helplessness and cynicism throughout the body politic. Hence, Bush's increased terror and security alerts and panic-inducing references to 9/11 are almost always framed in Manichean language of absolute good and evil. His doublespeak also employs the discourse of evangelicalism and its suggestion that whatever wisdom Bush has results from his direct communion with God—a position not unlike that of Moses on Mount Sinai, and which, of course, cannot be challenged by mere mortals.[40]

While all governments sometimes resort to misrepresentations and lies, Bush's doublespeak makes such action central to his government's maintenance of political power and its manipulation of the media and the public. Language is used in this context to say one thing, but to actually mean its opposite.[41] This type of discourse mimics George Orwell's dystopian world of *1984* where the Ministry of Truth actually produces lies and the Ministry of Love actually tortures people. Ruth Rosen emphasizes this point about Bush's Orwellian language. For instance, his Healthy Forest Initiative "allows increased logging of protected wilderness. The 'Clear Skies' initiative permits greater industrial air pollution."[42] With respect to the latter, the Bush administration has produced Spanish-language public service commercials hawking "Clear Skies" legislation, using ads that claim such legislation promotes "cleaner air," when, in fact, it has weakened restrictions on corporate polluters and eased regulations on some toxic emissions such as mercury. J.P. Suarez, the Environmental Protection Agency's chief of enforcement, recently notified his staff that "the agency would stop pursuing Clean Air Act enforcement cases against coal burning power plants."[43] Eric Pianin reported in *The Washington Post* that "The Bush administration has decided to allow thousands of the nation's dirtiest coal-fired power plants and refineries to upgrade their facilities without installing costly anti-pollution equipment as they now must do."[44] In addition, the Bush administration has weakened federal programs for cleaning up dirty waters and has removed from government reports scientific studies offering evidence of global warming.[45]

Even when it comes to children, Bush is undaunted in his use of deceptive language. In arguing for legislation that would shift financial responsibility to the states for the highly successful Head Start program, which provides over one million poor children with early educational, health, and nutrition services, Bush employed the phrase "opt in" to encourage Congress to pass new legislation reforming Head Start. While "opt in" sounds as if it refers to expanding the program, the phrase actually undermines Head Start because the states facing crushing deficits do not have the money to fund the programs. Thus, the legislation would drastically weaken Head Start. Such language calls to mind the Orwellian logic that "war is peace, freedom is slavery, and ignorance is strength."

There is also abundant evidence that the Bush administration manipulated intelligence to legitimate its claim for a pre-emptive war with Iraq. The list of misrepresentations and rhetorical contortions includes the claims that Iraq was building nuclear weapons, was engaged in the production of biological and chemical agents, and that Saddam Hussein was working with Osama bin Laden and had direct ties to Al Qaeda.[46] Even after the CIA reported that the charge that Saddam Hussein had bought uranium from the African country of Niger in pursuit of developing a nuclear weapon was fabricated, Bush included the assertion in his 2003 State of the Union Address.[47] As I mentioned in the last chapter, the Downing Street Memo, which consists of the actual minutes taken at a meeting with the British Prime Minister on July 23, 2000, recently leaked to *The Times* of London, makes it quite clear that the Bush administration completely fabricated a case for invading Iraq.[48]

Charges of Newspeak do not come exclusively from the Left or from cantankerous critics. *New York Times* op-ed writer and economist Paul Krugman asserts that "misrepresentation and deception are standard operating procedure for [the Bush] administration, which—to an extent never before seen in U.S. history—systematically and brazenly distorts the facts." And, in referring to Bush's record on selling the Iraqi war, he argues that it "is arguably the worst scandal in American political history—worse than Watergate, worse than Iran-contra. Indeed, the idea that we were deceived into war makes many commentators so uncomfortable that they refuse to admit the possibility."[49]

In what has to rank as one of the most egregious distortions (or maybe just delusional ravings, as the *New York Daily News* suggests)[50] that has emerged from the Bush administration, President Bush, in an interview with *New Yorker* reporter Ken Auletta, claimed that "No president has ever done more for human rights than I have."[51] Such a statement is extraordinary, given that Amnesty International condemned the United

States in 2002 for being one of the world leaders in human rights violations. Similarly, organizations such as Human Rights Watch, US Human
Rights Network, the ACLU, the Center for Constitutional Rights, and
Amnesty International have accused the Bush administration itself of engaging in various human rights violations, including: preventing foreign
nationals held as prisoners at Guantanamo Bay from gaining access to US
courts; executing juvenile offenders; engaging in racial profiling, detention, inhumane treatment, and deportation of Muslim immigrants after
September 11, 2001; and refusing to ratify the American Convention on
Human Rights, the Geneva Conventions, the International Covenant on
Civil and Political Rights, the Convention on the Rights of the Child,
and numerous other international agreements aimed at protecting human
rights.

A sixth element of proto-fascism is the growing collapse of the
separation between the church and state, on the one hand, and the increasing use of religious rhetoric as a marker of political identity and the shaping
of public policy, on the other. Religion has always played a powerful role
in the daily lives of Americans, but it has never wielded such influence in
the highest levels of American government as it does under the Bush presidency. Moreover, the religious conservative movement that has come into
political prominence with the election of George W. Bush views him as its
earthly leader. As *Washington Post* staff writer Dana Milibank, puts it:

> For the first time since religious conservatism became a mod-
> ern political movement, the president of the United States has

become the movement's de facto leader—a status even Ronald Reagan, though admired by religious conservatives, never earned. Christian publications, radio and television shower Bush with praise, while preachers from the pulpit treat his leadership as an act of providence. A procession of religious leaders who have met with him testify to his faith, while Web sites encourage people to fast and pray for the president. [52]

Considered the leader of the Christian Right, Bush is viewed by many of his aides and followers as a leader with a higher purpose. Bush aide Tim Goeglein echoes this view: "I think President Bush is God's man at this hour, and I say this with a great sense of humility."[53] Ralph Reed, a long-time crusader against divorce, single-parent families, and abortion, and current head of Georgia's Republican Party, assesses Bush's relationship with the Christian Right in more sobering political terms. He argues that the role of the religious conservative movement has changed in that it is no longer on the outskirts of power since it has helped to elect leaders who believe in its cause. Referring to the newfound role of the religious Right, he claims, "You're no longer throwing rocks at the building; you're in the building."[54] Bush has not disappointed his radical evangelical Christian following.

Believing he is on a direct mission from God, President Bush openly celebrates the virtues of evangelical Christian morality, prays daily, and expresses his fervent belief in Christianity in both his rhetoric and policy choices. For example, while running as a presidential candidate in 2000, Bush proclaimed that his favourite philosopher was Jesus Christ.

Further, in a speech in which he outlined the dangers posed by Iraq, he stated, "We do not claim to know all the ways of Providence, yet we can trust in them, placing our confidence in the loving God behind all of life, and all of history. May He guide us now."[55] In his book *The Faith of George W. Bush*, Stephen Mansfield claims that Bush told James Robinson, a Texas preacher: "I feel like God wants me to run for president. I can't explain it, but I sense my country is going to need me. ... I know it won't be easy on me or my family, but God wants me to do it."[56] Asked by Bob Woodward if he had consulted with his father about invading Iraq, President Bush replied, "There is a higher father that I appeal to."[57] Surrounded by born-again missionaries and relying on God, rather than the most basic tenets of American democracy to provide a source of leadership, Bush has relentlessly developed policies based less on social needs than on a highly personal and narrowly moral sense of divine purpose. Using the privilege of executive action, he has aggressively attempted to evangelize the realm of social services. For example, he has made available, to a greater extent than any other president, more federal funds to Christian religious groups for them to provide a range of social services. He has also eased the rules "for overtly religious institutions to access $20-billion in federal social service grants and another $8-billion in Housing and Urban Development money. Tax dollars can now be used to construct and renovate houses of worship as long as the funds are not used to build the principal room used for prayer, such as the sanctuary or chapel."[58] He also provided more than $60 billion in federal funds for faith-based initiatives organized by religious charitable groups.[59] Not all religious groups, however, receive equal funding. The lion's share of federal monies goes to Christian organizations, thus undermining, via state sanction of some religions over others, the very idea of religious freedom. In addition, he has promised that such agencies can get government funds "without being forced to change their character or compromise their mission."[60] This means that such organizations and groups can now get federal money even if they discriminate on religious grounds in their hiring practices. The only two programs that Bush showcased during his January 2003 State of the Union Address both "use religious conversion as treatment."[61] Bush has also created an office in the White House entirely dedicated to providing assistance to faith-based organizations applying for federal funding. Moreover, he is using school voucher programs to enable private schools to receive public money and refusing to fund schools that "interfere with or fail to accommodate prayer for bible study by teachers or students."[62] The then Secretary of Education, Rod Paige, made it clear how he feels about the separation of church and state when he told a Baptist publication that he believed that schools should teach Christian values. When asked to resign by a number of critics, Paige refused and his office declined to clarify, let alone repudiate, his suggestion that either public schools should teach Christian values or parents should take their kids out of such schools and send them to parochial schools. His office replied curtly: "The quotes are the quotes."[63] The Bush administration has also refused to sign a United Nations Declaration on Children's Rights unless it eliminates sexual health services such as providing teenagers with sex education in which contraception or reproductive rights are discussed. On the domestic front, Bush passed legislation halting "late-term" abortion, tried to pass legislation stopping the distribution of the morning-after pill, and eliminated financial support for international charities that provide advice on abortion. Such measures not only call into question the traditional separation between church and state; they also undercut public services and provide a veneer of government legitimacy to religious-based organizations that give priority to religious conversion over modern scientific techniques. As Winnifred Sullivan, a senior lecturer at the University of Chicago Divinity School puts it, the conservative evangelical proponents of the faith-based initiative "want government funds to go to the kinds of churches that regard conversion as part of your rehabilitation. It's a critique of secular professional social service standards."[64]

Unfortunately, Bush's religious fervour appears more indebted to the God of the Old Testament, the God who believes in an eye for an eye, the God of vengeance and retribution. Hence, Bush appears indifferent to the seeming contradiction between his claim to religious piety and his willingness, as the governor of Texas, to execute "more prisoners (152) than any governor in modern U.S. history."[65] Nor does he see the contradiction between upholding the word of God and imposing democracy on the largely Muslim population of Iraq through the rule of force and the barrel of a gun. Indeed, while Bush and his religious cohorts claim they are working to exercise great acts of charity, it appears that the poor are being punished, and the only charity available is the handout being given to the rich.

For instance, as funds were being distributed for faith-based initiatives, Congress not only passed legislation that eliminated a child tax credit that would have benefitted about two million children; it also agreed to a $350 billion tax cut for the rich while slashing domestic spending for programs that benefit the poor, the elderly, and children.

Bush is not the only one in his administration who combines evangelical morality with dubious ethical actions and undemocratic practices. Former Attorney General John Ashcroft, a Christian fundamentalist who held morning prayer sessions in his Washington office, added another layer to this type of religious fervour in February 2002 when he told a crowd at the National Religious Broadcasters Convention in Nashville, Tennessee, that the freedoms Americans enjoy appear to have little to do with the men who wrote the US Constitution, since such freedoms are made in heaven. Ashcroft argues that "We are a nation called to defend freedom—a freedom that is not the grant of any government or document but is our endowment from God."[66] Without any irony intended, Ashcroft further exhibited his rigid Christian morality by having the "Spirit of Justice" statue draped so as to cover up her marble breasts while, at the same time, violating the constitutional rights of thousands of Muslims and Arabs whom, since September 11, 2001, he has arrested, detained in secret, and offered no legal recourse or access to their families. Such harsh treatment rooted in a Manichean notion of absolute good and evil represents more than an act of capricious justice; it also undermines "the presumption of innocence, as well as the constitutional rights to due process, to counsel, and to a speedy and public trial." In legitimating such treatment, "the Bush administration has weak-ened these protections for all, citizens and aliens alike. In the process, it has tarnished American democracy."[67]

Behind the rhetoric of religious commitment is the reality of per-manent war, the further disadvantaging of the poor, and the ongoing at-tacks on the notion of the secular state. There is also the force of intolerance and bigotry, and the refusal to recognize the multiplicity of religious, politi-cal, linguistic, and cultural differences—those vast and diverse elements that constitute the democratic global sphere at its best. Hints of this bigotry are visible not only in the culture of fear and religious fundamentalism that shapes the world of Bush and his aides, but also in those who serve them with unquestioning loyalty. This became clear when the national press re-vealed that a high-ranking Defense Department official called the war on terrorism a "Christian battle against Satan." Lt. General William Boykin, in his capacity as Deputy Under Secretary of Defense for Intelligence, while standing in front of pictures of Osama bin Laden, Saddam Hus-sein, and Kim Jong Il, asked the parishioners of the First Baptist Church of Broken Arrow, Oklahoma, the following question: "Why do they hate us? … The answer to that is because we are a Christian nation. We are hated because we are a nation of believers." He continued, "Our spiritual enemy will only be defeated if we come against them in the name of Jesus."[68] For Boykin, the war being fought in Iraq, Afghanistan, and maybe eventually at home against other non-believers, is a holy war. Boykin appears to be serious when claiming that other countries "have lost their morals, lost their values. But America is still a Christian nation."[69] This language is not merely the ranting of a religious fanatic; it is symptomatic of a deeper strain of intolerance and authoritarianism that is emerging in the US. It can be heard in the words of Reverend Jerry Falwell, who claimed on the airwaves that the terrorist attack of 9/11 was the result of God's judgement on the secularizing of America. He stated: "I really believe that the pagans, and the abortionists, and the feminists, and the gays and lesbians, the ACLU, People for the American Way—all of them who have tried to secularize America—I point the finger in their face and say, 'You helped this happen.'"[70] It can be heard in the diatribes of the founder of the Christian Coalition, Pat Robertson, who argues that Islam is not a peaceful religion, and in the claims of many other Christian fundamentalists in America. The emergence of a government-sanctioned religious fundamentalism has its counterpart in a political authoritarianism that undermines not only the most basic tenets of religious faith, but also the democratic tenets of social justice and equality. Of course, this type of religious fundamentalism, supported largely by politicians and evangelical missionaries who run to the prayer groups and Bible study cells sprouting up all over the Bush White House, has little to do with genuine religion or spirituality. Those who believe that biblical creationism rather than evolution should be taught in the schools, or that the United States "must extend God's will of liberty for other countries, by force if necessary,"[71] do not represent the prophetic traditions in Islam, Christianity, or Judaism. These traditions foster belief in a God who is giving and compassionate, who rejects secular policies that bankrupt the government in order to benefit the rich or that produce laws that disadvantage the poor and impose more suffering on those already in need. They are traditions espoused by the Reverend James Forbes Jr., head of the Riverside Church in New York City, and captured in his assertion that "poverty is a weapon of mass destruction."[72] Joseph Hough, the head of Union Theological Seminary, speaks for many religious leaders when he argues that what passes as Christianity in the Bush administration is simply a form of political machination masquerading as religion and making a grab for power. He writes:

> I'm getting tired of people claiming they're carrying the banner of my religious tradition when they're doing everything possible to undercut it. And that's what's happening in this country right now. The policies of this country are disadvantaging poor people every day of our lives and every single thing that passes the Congress these days is disadvantaging poor people more ... And anybody who claims in the name of God they're gonna run over people of other nations, and just willy-nilly, by your own free will, reshape the world in your own image, and claim that you're acting on behalf of God, that sounds a lot like Caesar to me.[73]

Apocalyptic Biblical prophesies fuel more than the likes of John Ashcroft, who opposes dancing on moral grounds, or David Hager, appointed by Bush to the FDA's Advisory Committee for Reproductive Health Drugs, "who refuses to prescribe contraceptives to unmarried women (and believes the Bible is an antidote for premenstrual syndrome);"[74] they also fuel a world view in which immigrants, African-Americans, and others marked by differences in class, race, gender, and nationality are demonized, scapegoated, and subjected to acts of state violence. Such rhetoric and the policies it supports must be recognized as a crisis of democracy itself. What progressives and others must acknowledge is that the Bush administration's attempt to undo the separation between church and state is driven by a form of fundamentalism that both discredits democratic values, public goods, and critical citizenship, and spawns an irrationality evident in the innumerable contradictions between its rhetoric of "compassionate conservative" religious commitment and its relentless grab for economic and political power—an irrationality that is the hallmark of both the old fascism and proto-fascism.

While there are other elements central to proto-fascism, I want to conclude in substantial detail with a discussion of the growing militarization of public space and of the social order in American society. Of course, the militarization of public space was a central feature of the old fascism. This feature is particularly important in the United States today because it poses the greatest risk to our civil liberties and to any semblance of democracy, and it has been a crucial force in the rise of the national security state.

The Politics of Militarization at Home and Abroad

"Militarization" refers to the related instances of the centrality of the military in American society, the militarization of US culture, and the increased propensity to suppress dissent. The process of militarization has a long history in the United States and is varied rather than static, changing under different historical conditions.[75] The militarizing of public space at home contributes to the narrowing of community and a growing escalation of concentrated, unaccountable political power that threatens the foundation of democracy in the United States. Militarization is no longer simply the driving force of foreign policy; it has become a defining principle for social changes at home. Catherine Lutz captures the multiple registers and complex processes of militarization that have extensively shaped social life during the twentieth century:

> By militarization, I mean ... an intensification of the labor and resources allocated to military purposes, including the shaping of other institutions in synchrony with military goals. Militarization is simultaneously a discursive process, involving a shift in general societal beliefs and values in ways necessary to legitimate the use of force, the organization of large standing armies and their leaders, and the higher taxes or tribute used to pay for them. Militarization is intimately connected not only to the obvious increase in the size of armies and resurgence of militant nationalisms and militant fundamentalisms but also to the less visible deformation of human potentials into the hierarchies of race, class, gender, and sexuality, and to the shaping of national histories in ways that glorify and legitimate military action.[76]

Lutz's definition of militarization is inclusive, attentive to its discursive, ideological, and material relations of power in the service of war and violence. But militarization is also a strong cultural politics that works its way through everyday life, spawning particular notions of masculinity, sanctioning war as a spectacle and fear as a central, formative component in mobilizing an effective investment in militarization. In other words, the forces of militarization, with their emphasis on the discursive production of violence and the material practices it entails, have produced a pervasive *culture* of militarization, which "inject[s] a constant military presence in our lives."[77] Unlike the old style of militarization in which all forms of civil authority are subordinate to military authority, the new ethos of militarization is organized to engulf the entire social order, legitimating its own values as a central rather than peripheral aspect of American public life. Moreover, the values of militarism no longer reside in a single group nor are they limited to a particular sphere of society. On the contrary, Jorge Mariscal points out:

> In liberal democracies, in particular, the values of militarism do not reside in a single group but are diffused across a wide variety of cultural locations. In twenty-first century America, no one is exempt from militaristic values because the processes of militarization allow those values to permeate the fabric of everyday life.[78]

The growing influence of the military presence and ideology in American society is evident, in part, since the United States has more police, prisons, spies, weapons, and soldiers than at any other time in its history. This radical shift in the size, scope, and influence of the military can be seen in the redistribution of domestic resources and government funding away from social programs into military-oriented security measures at home and into war abroad. As Richard Falk has pointed out, "The US Government is devoting huge resources to the monopolistic militarization of space, the development of more usable nuclear weapons, and the strengthening of its world-girdling ring of military bases and its global navy, as the most tangible way to discourage any strategic challenges to its preeminence."[79] According to journalist George Monbiot, the US government "is now spending as much on war as it is on education, public health, housing, employment, pensions, food aid and welfare put together."[80] On the other hand, the state is being radically transformed into a national security state, increasingly under the sway of the military-corporate-industrial-educational complex. The military logic of fear, surveillance, and control is gradually permeating our public schools, universities, streets, popular culture, and criminal justice system.

Since the events of 9/11 and the wars in Afghanistan and Iraq, the military has assumed a privileged place in American society. President Bush not only celebrates the military presence in American culture, he cultivates it by going out of his way to give speeches at military facilities, talk to military personnel, and address veterans groups. He often wears a military uniform when speaking to "captive audiences at military bases, defense plants, and on aircraft carriers."[81] He also takes advantage of the campaign value of military culture by using military symbolism as a political prop to attract the widest possible media attention. One glaring instance occurred on May 1, 2003, when Bush landed in full aviator flight uniform on the USS *Abraham Lincoln* in the Pacific Ocean, where he officially proclaimed the end of the Iraq war. There was also his secret trip to Baghdad to spend Thanksgiving Day (2003) with the troops, an event that attracted world-wide coverage in all the media. But Bush has done more than take advantage of the military as a campaign prop to sell his domestic and foreign policies. His administration and the Republican Party, which now controls all three branches of government, have developed a new, potentially dangerous, "and unprecedented confluence of our democratic institutions and the military."[82] Writing in *Harper's* magazine, Kevin Baker claims that the military "has become the most revered institution in the country."[83] Soon after the Iraqi War, a Gallup poll reported that over 76 percent of Americans "expressed 'a great deal' or 'quite a lot' of confidence in their nation's military." Among a poll of 1200 students conducted by Harvard University, 75 percent believed that the military, most of the time, would "do the right thing." In addition, the students "characterized themselves as hawks over doves by a ratio of two to one."[84]

Popular fears about domestic safety and internal threats, accentuated by endless terror alerts, have created a society that increasingly accepts the notion of a "war without limits" as a normal state of affairs. But fear and insecurity do more than produce a collective anxiety among Americans, exploited largely to convince them that they should vote Republican because it is the only political party that can protect them. In addition to producing manufactured political loyalty, such fears can also be manipulated into a kind of "war fever." The mobilization of war fever, intensified through a politics of fear, carries with it a kind of paranoid edge, endlessly stoked by government alerts and repressive laws, and used "to create the most extensive national security apparatus in our nation's history."[85] But war fever is also reproduced in the Foxified media, which—in addition to constantly marketing the flag and implying that critics of American foreign policy are traitors—offer up seemingly endless images of brave troops on the front line, heroic stories of released American prisoners, and utterly privatized commentaries on those wounded or killed in battle.[86] *Time Magazine* embodied this representational indulgence in military culture by naming "The American Soldier" as the "Person of the Year" for 2003. Not only have such ongoing and largely uncritical depictions of war injected a constant military presence in American life, they have also helped to create a civil society that has become more aggressive in its warlike enthusiasms. But there is more at work here than the exploitation of the troops for higher ratings, or the attempts by right-wing political strategists to keep the American public in a state of permanent fear so as to remove pressing domestic issues from public debate. There is also the attempt by the Bush administration to convince as many Americans as possible that under the current "state of emergency," the use of the military internally in domestic affairs is perfectly acceptable. There is an increasing propensity to use the military establishment "to incarcerate and interrogate suspected terrorists and 'enemy combatants' and keep them beyond the reach of the civilian judicial system, even if they are American citizens."[87] It is also evident in the federal government's attempt to try terrorists in military courts and to detain prisoners "outside the provisions of the Geneva Convention as prisoners of war. . . . at the US. Marine Corps base at Guantanamo, Cuba, because that facility is outside of the reach of the American courts."[88]

Militarization abroad cannot be separated from the increasing militarization of society at home. War takes on a new meaning in American life as wars are waged on drugs, social policies are criminalized, youth are tried as adults, incarceration rates soar among the poor, especially people of colour, and schools are increasingly modelled after prisons. Citizens are recruited as foot soldiers in the war on terrorism, urged to spy on their neighbours' behaviors, watch for suspicious-looking people, and supply data to government sources in the war on terrorism. Major universities more intensively court the military establishment for defense department grants and, in doing so, become less open to academic subjects or programs that encourage rigourous debate and critical thinking. As a result of the No Child Left Behind Act, President Bush's educational law, "schools risk losing all federal aid if they fail to provide military recruiters full access to their students; the aid is contingent with complying with federal law."[89] Schools were once viewed as democratic public spheres that would teach students how to resist the militarization of democratic life, or at least to learn the skills to peacefully engage domestic and international problems. Now they serve as recruiting stations for students to fight enemies at home and abroad.

Schools represent one of the most serious public spheres to come under the influence of military culture and values. Tough love now translates into zero-tolerance policies that turn public schools into prison-like institutions, as students' rights diminish under the onslaught of a military-like imposed discipline. Students in many schools, especially those in poor urban areas, are routinely searched, frisked, subjected to involuntary drug tests, maced, and carted off to jail. In a report on schools in New York City, Elissa Gootman claims, "In some places, schools are resorting to zero-tolerance policies that put students in handcuffs for dress code violations."[90]

As educators turn over their responsibility for school safety to the police, the new security culture in public schools has turned them into "learning prisons,"[91] most evident in the ways in which schools are being "reformed" through the addition of armed guards, barbed-wired security fences, and lock-down drills. In Goose Creek, South Carolina, police conducted an early morning drug-sweep at Stratford High School. When the police arrived, they drew guns on students, handcuffed them, and made them kneel facing the wall.[92] No drugs were found in the raid. Though this incident was aired on the national news, there were few protests from the public.

But children, schools, and popular culture are not the only victims of a growing militarization of American society. The civil rights of people of colour and immigrants, especially Arabs and Muslims, are being violated, often resulting in either imprisonment, deportation, or government harassment. All this is happening in the name of anti-terrorism laws used by the Bush administration to justify abusive military campaigns abroad and to stifle dissent at home. Government measures to combat terrorism now support an arms budget that is larger than that of all other major industrialized countries combined. Similarly, as Jeremy Brecher points out,

> the escalating rhetoric of the "War against Terrorism" to the "Axis of Evil" has provided a model for belligerence and potentially for nuclear conflict from India and Pakistan to Israel and Palestine. This militarization of conflict has been justified by the terroristic attacks against the United States, but as a *New York Times* editorial pointed out, "Bush is using the anti-terrorism campaign to disguise an ideological agenda that it has nothing to do with domestic defense or battling terrorism abroad."[93]

What is, in fact, being labelled as a war against terrorism waged by outsiders against the United States is increasingly beginning to look like a war waged by the Bush administration against democracy itself.

The rampant combination of fear and insecurity, so much a part of the permanent war culture in the United States, seems to bear down particularly hard on children. In many poor school districts, specialists are being laid off and crucial mental health services are being cut back. As Sara Rimer pointed out in the *New York Times*, much-needed student-based services and traditional, if not compassionate, ways of dealing with student problems are now being replaced by the juvenile justice system, which functions "as a dumping ground for poor minority kids with mental health and special-education problems. ... The juvenile detention center has become an extension of the principal's office."[94] For example, in some cities, ordinances have been passed that "allow for the filing of misdemeanor charges against students for anything from disrupting a class to assaulting a teacher."[95] Children are no longer given a second chance for minor behaviour infractions, nor are they sent to the guidance counsellor, the principal, or to detention. They now come under the jurisdiction of the courts and juvenile justice system.

The militarization of public high schools has become so commonplace that even in the face of the most flagrant disregard for children's rights, such acts are justified by administrators and by the public on the grounds that they keep kids safe. In Biloxi, Mississippi, surveillance cameras have been installed in all its 500 classrooms. The school's administrators call this "school reform" but none of them has examined the implications of what they are teaching kids who are put under constant surveillance. The not-so-hidden curriculum here is that kids can't be trusted and that their rights are not worth protecting. At the same time, they are being educated to passively accept military-sanctioned practices that maintain control, surveillance, and unquestioned authority, all conditions central to a police state and proto-fascism. It gets worse. Some schools are actually using sting operations in which undercover agents pretend to be students in order to catch young people suspected of selling drugs or committing any one of a number of school infractions. The consequences of such actions are far-reaching. As Randall Beger points out:

> Opponents of school-based sting operations say they not only create a climate of mistrust between students and police, but they also put innocent students at risk of wrongful arrest due to faulty tips and overzealous police work. When asked about his role in a recent undercover probe at a high school near Atlanta, a young-looking police officer who attended classes and went to

71

parties with students replied: "I knew I had to fit in, make kids trust me and then turn around and take them to jail."[96]

Instances of domestic militarization and the war at home can also be seen in the rise of the prison-industrial-educational complex and the militarization of the criminal justice system. The traditional "distinctions between military, police, and criminal justice are blurring."[97] The police now work in close collaboration with the military. This takes the form of receiving surplus weapons, arranging technology/information transfers, introducing SWAT teams modelled after the Navy Seals—which are experiencing a steep growth in police departments throughout the US—and becoming more dependent on military models of crime control.[98] The increasing use of military models in American life has played a crucial role in paramilitarizing the culture, which provides both a narrative and legitimation "for recent trends in corrections, including the normalization of special response teams, the increasingly popular Supermax prisons, and drug war boot camps."[99] In the paramilitaristic perspective, crime is no longer a social problem. Crime is now both an individual pathology and a matter of punishment, rather than rehabilitation. Unsurprisingly, paramilitary culture embodies a racist and class-specific discourse and "reflects the discrediting of the social and its related narratives."[100] This is particularly evident as America's inner cities are being singled out as dangerous enclaves of crime and violence. The consequences for those communities have been catastrophic, especially in terms of the rise of the prison-industrial complex. The United States is now the biggest jailer in the world. Between 1985 and

2002, the prison population grew from 744,206 to 2.1 million (approaching the combined populations of Idaho, Wyoming, and Montana), and prison budgets jumped from seven billion dollars in 1980 to forty billion dollars in 2000.[101] Sanho Tree points out:

> With more than 2 million people behind bars (there are only 8 million prisoners in the entire world), the United States—with one-twenty-second of the world's population—has one-quarter of the planet's prisoners. We operate the largest penal system in the world, and approximately one quarter of all our prisoners (nearly half a million people) are there for nonviolent drug offenses.[102]

Yet, even as the crime rate plummets dramatically, more people, especially those of colour, are being arrested, harassed, punished, and put in jail.[103] Of the two million people behind bars, 70 percent of the inmates are people of colour: 50 percent are African American and 17 percent are Latino.[104] A justice department report points out that, on any given day in the US, "more than a third of the young African-American men aged 18-34 in some of our major cities are either in prison or under some form of criminal justice supervision."[105] The same department reported in April 2000 that "black youth are forty-eight times more likely than whites to be sentenced to juvenile prison for drug offenses."[106] When poor youth of colour are not being warehoused in dilapidated schools or incarcerated, they are being aggressively recruited by the army to fight the war in Iraq. For example, Carl Chery reported:

> With help from *The Source* magazine, the U.S. military is target-
> ing hip-hop fans with custom made Hummers, throwback jer-
> seys and trucker hats. The yellow Hummer, spray-painted with
> two black men in military uniform, is the vehicle of choice for
> the U.S. Army's "Take It to the Streets campaign"—a sponsored
> mission aimed at recruiting young African Americans into the
> military ranks.[107]

It seems that the Army has discovered hip-hop and urban culture and,
rather than listening to their searing indictments of poverty, joblessness,
and despair, the Army's recruiters appeal to their most commodified elements by letting the "potential recruits hang out in the Hummer, where
they can pep the sound system or watch recruitment videos."[108] Of course,
they won't view any videos of Hummers being blown up in the war-torn
streets of Baghdad.

Under the auspices of the national security state and the militarization of domestic life, containment policies become the principal means to
discipline working-class youth and restrict their ability to think critically
and engage in oppositional practices. Marginalized students learn quickly
that they are surplus populations and that the journey from home to school
no longer means they will next move into a job; on the contrary, school
now becomes a training ground for their "graduation" into containment
centres such as prisons and jails that keep them out of sight, patrolled, and
monitored so as to prevent them from becoming a social canker or political
liability to those white and middle-class populations concerned about their
own safety. Schools increasingly function as zoning mechanisms to separate

students marginalized by class and colour, and, as such, these institutions are now modelled after prisons. David Garland points out that "Large-scale incarceration functions as a mode of economic and social placement, a zoning mechanism that segregates those populations rejected by the depleted institutions of family, work, and welfare and places them behind the scenes of social life."[109]

Judging from Bush's 2005 State of the Union Address, the Bush administration will continue to allocate funds for an "educational reform" policy intended to strip young people of the capacity to think critically by teaching them that learning is largely about test taking, and by preparing them for a culture in which punishment has become the central principle of reform. Bush cannot fully fund his own educational reform act, but he pledged in his 2005 State of the Union address an additional twenty-three million dollars to promote drug testing in public schools. In short, fear, punishment, and containment continue to override the need to provide health care for 9.3 million uninsured children, as well as the need to increase the ranks of new teachers by at least 100,000, fully support Head Start programs, repair deteriorating schools, and improve those youth services that, for many poor students, would provide an alternative to the direct pipeline between school and the local police station, the courts, or prison.

Domestic militarization, also widespread in the realm of culture, functions as a mode of public pedagogy, instilling the values and the aesthetic of militarization through a wide variety of pedagogical sites and cultural venues. For instance, one of the fastest-growing sports for middle-class suburban youth is the game of paintball, "in which teenagers stalk and shoot each other on 'battlefields.' (In San Diego, paintball participants pay an additional $50 to hone their skills at the Camp Pendleton Marine Base)."[110] And military recruitment ads flood all modes of entertainment, using sophisticated marketing tools with messages that have a strong appeal to the hyper-masculinity of young men and resonate powerfully with the enticement for recruitment. For example, the Web site, www.marines.com, opens with the sound of gunfire and then provides the following message:

> We are the warriors, one and all. Born to defend, built to conquer. The steel we wear is the steel within ourselves, forged by the hot fires of discipline and training. We are fierce in a way no other can be. We are the marines.

In popular culture, video games such as *Doom* have a long history of using violent graphics and shooting techniques that appeal to the most hyper-modes of masculinity. The Marine Corps was so taken with *Doom* in the mid-1990s that it produced its own version of the game, *Marine Doom*, and made it available to download for free. One of the developers of the game, Lieutenant Scott Barnett, claimed at the time that it was a useful game to keep marines entertained. The interface of military and popular culture is not only valuable in providing video-game technology for diverse military uses; it has also resulted in the armed forces' developing partnerships "with the video game industry to train and recruit soldiers."[111] The video-game makers offer products that have the imprimatur of a first-class fighting machine. And the popularity of militarized war games is on the rise. Nick Turse argues that as the line between entertainment and war disappears, a "'military-entertainment complex' [has] sprung up to feed both the military's desire to bring out ever-more-realistic computer and video combat games. Through video games, the military and its partners in academia and the entertainment industry are creating an arm of media culture geared toward preparing young Americans for armed conflict."[112] Combat teaching games offer a perfect link between the Pentagon, with its accelerating military budget, and the entertainment industry, with annual revenues of $479 billion, including $40 billion from the video-game industry. The entertainment industry offers a stamp of approval for the Pentagon's war games, and the Defense Department provides an aura of authenticity for corporate America's war-based products. Collaboration between the Defense Department and the entertainment industry has been going on since 1997, but the permanent war culture that now grips the United States has given this partnership a new life and has greatly expanded its presence in popular culture.

The military has found numerous ways to take advantage of the intersection between popular culture and the new electronic technologies. Such technologies are being employed not only to train military personnel, but also to attract recruits, tapping into the realm of popular culture's celebration of video games, computer technology, the Internet, and other elements used by teenagers.[113] For instance, the army has developed on-line software that appeals to computer-literate recruits, the most attractive feature being a shooting game "that actually simulates battle and strategic-warfare situations."[114] When asked about the violence being portrayed, Brian Ball, the lead developer of the game, was clear about the purpose of the video: "We don't downplay the fact that the Army manages violence. We hope that this will help people understand the role of the military in American life."[115]

Capitalizing on its link with industry, the military now has a host of new war games in production. For instance, there is *America's Army*, one of the most popular and successful recruiting video games. This game teaches young people how "to kill enemy soldiers while wearing your pajamas [and also provides] plenty of suggestions about visiting your local recruiter and joining the real US Army."[116] Using the most updated versions of satellite technology, military-industry collaboration has also produced *Kuma: War*, developed by the Department of Defense and Kuma Reality Games, and released in 2004. It is a subscription-based product that "prepares gamers for actual missions based on real-world conflicts."[117] Updated weekly, the game allows players to recreate actual news stories such as the raid American forces conducted in Mosul, Iraq, in which Saddam Hussein's two sons, Uday and Qusay, were killed. Gamers can take advantage of real "true to life satellite imagery and authentic military intelligence, to jump from the headlines right into the frontlines of international conflict."[118] Of course, the realities of carrying thirty-six-kilogram knapsacks in 120-degree heat, dealing with the panic-inducing anxiety and fear of real people shooting real bullets or planting real bombs to kill or maim you and your fellow soldiers, and spending months, if not years, away from family, are not among those experiences reproduced for instruction or entertainment.

Young people no longer learn military values in training camp or in military-oriented schools. These values are now disseminated through the pedagogical force of popular culture itself, which has become a major tool used by the armed forces to educate young people about the ideology and social relations that inform military life—minus a few of the unpleasantries. The collaboration between the military and the entertainment industry offers a form of public pedagogy that "may help to produce great battlefield decision makers, but ... strikes from debate the most crucial decisions young people can make in regard to the morality of a war—choosing whether or not to fight and for what cause."[119]

Along with the militaristic transformation of the country, attitudes toward war play have changed dramatically, resulting in the major increase in the sales, marketing, and consumption of military toys, games, videos, and clothing. Corporations recognize that there are big profits to be made from the upsurge in patriotic jingoism at a time when military symbolism gets a boost from the war in Iraq. The popularity of militarized culture is also apparent in the sales of children's toys. Major retailers and major chain stores across the country are selling out of war-related toys. KB Toys stores in San Antonio, Texas, sold out in one day an entire shipment of fatigue-clad, plush hamsters that dance to military music, and managers at KB Toys were instructed "to feature military toys in the front of their stores."[120] Sales of action figures have also soared. Hasbro reported that "between 2001 and 2002, sales of *G.I. Joe* increased by 46 percent. And when toy retailer Small Blue Planet launched a series of figures called Special Forces: Showdown with Iraq, two of the four models sold out immediately."[121] Japanese electronic giant SONY attempted to cash in on the war in Iraq by patenting the phrase "Shock and Awe" for use with video and computer games. The phrase, coined by Pentagon strategists as part of a scare tactic to be used against Iraq, referred to the massive air bombardment planned for Baghdad in the initial stages of the war. In addition, the *New York Times* reported that after September 11, 2001, "nearly two dozen applications were filed for the phrase, 'Let's Roll,'" the term made famous by one of the passengers on the ill-fated abducted plane that crashed in a field in Pennsylvania.

Even in the world of fashion, the chic of militarization and patriotism makes its mark. Army-Navy stores are doing a brisk business selling American flags, gas masks, aviator sunglasses, night-vision goggles, other military equipment, and also clothing with the camouflage look.[122] Even top designers are getting into the act—at a recent fashion show in Milan, Italy, many designers were "drawn to G.I. uniforms [and were] fascinated by the construction of military uniforms." One designer "had beefy models in commando gear scramble over tabletops and explode balloons."[123]

Proto-fascism views life as a form of permanent warfare and, in doing so, subordinates society to the military, rather than viewing the military as subordinate to the needs of a democratic social order. Militarism in this scenario diminishes both the legitimate reasons for a military presence in society and the necessary struggle for the promise of democracy itself. As Umberto Eco points out, proto-fascist ideology under the rubric of its aggressive militarism maintains that "there is no struggle for life but, rather, life is lived for struggle."[124] The ideology of militarization is central to any understanding of proto-fascism since it appeals to a form of irrationality at odds with any viable notion of democracy. Militarization uses fear to drive human behaviour, and the values it promotes are mainly distrust, patriarchy, and intolerance. Within this ideology, masculinity is associated with violence, and action is often substituted for the democratic processes of deliberation and debate. Militarization as an ideology is about the rule of force and the expansion of repressive state power. In fact, democracy appears as an excess in this logic and is often condemned by militarists as being a weak system of government.

Echoes of this anti-democratic sentiment can be found in the passage of the USA PATRIOT Act with its violation of civil liberties, in the rancorous patriotism that equates dissent with treason, and in the discourse of public commentators who, in the fervour of a militarized culture, fan the flames of hatred and intolerance. One example that has become all too typical emerged after the September 11th attacks. Columnist Ann Coulter, in calling for a holy war on Muslims, wrote, "We should invade their countries, kill their leaders and convert them to Christianity. We weren't punctilious about locating and punishing only Hitler and his top officers. We carpet-bombed German cities; we killed civilians. That's war. And this is war."[125] While this statement does not reflect mainstream American opinion, the uncritical and chauvinistic patriotism and intolerance that inform it have become standard fare, not only among many conservative radio hosts in the United States, but increasingly in a wide variety of cultural venues. As militarization spreads through the culture, it produces policies that rely more on force than on dialogue and compassion, it offers up modes of identification that undermine democratic values and tarnish civil liberties, and it makes the production of both symbolic and material violence a central feature of everyday life. As Kevin Baker points out, we are quickly becoming a nation that "substitute[s] military solutions for almost everything, including international alliances, diplomacy, effective intelligence agencies, democratic institutions—even national security."[126] By blurring the lines between military and civilian functions, militarization deforms our language, debases democratic values, celebrates fascist modes of control, defines citizens as soldiers, and diminishes our ability as a nation to uphold international law and support a democratic global public sphere. Unless militarization is systematically exposed and resisted whenever it appears in the culture, it will undermine the meaning of critical citizenship and do great harm to institutions central to a democratic society.

Neoliberalism and the Death of Democracy

I submit that neo-liberalism has changed the fundamental nature of politics. Politics used to be primarily about who ruled whom and who got what share of the pie. Aspects of both these central questions remain, of course, but the great new central question of politics is, in my view, "Who has a right to live and who does not." Radical exclusion is now the order of the day, and I mean this deadly seriously.[127]

It is impossible to understand the rise of such multi-faceted authoritarianism in American society without analyzing the importance of neoliberalism as the defining ideology of the current historical moment.[128] Although fascism does not need neoliberalism to develop, neoliberalism creates the ideological and economic conditions that can promote a uniquely American version of fascism.[129] Neoliberalism not only undermines vital economic and political institutions and public spaces central to a democracy, it also has no vocabulary for recognizing anti-democratic forms of power. Even worse, it accentuates a structural relationship between the state and the economy that produces hierarchies of accumulation, concentrates power in relatively few hands, unleashes the most brutal elements of a rabid individualism, destroys the welfare state, incarcerates large numbers of its disposable population, economically disenfranchises large segments of the lower and middle classes, and reduces entire countries to poverty.[130]

Under neoliberalism, the state now makes a grim alignment with corporate capital and transnational corporations. Gone are the days when the state "assumed responsibility for a range of social needs."[131] Instead, agencies of government now pursue a wide range of "'deregulations,' privatizations, and abdications of responsibility to the market and private philanthropy."[132] Deregulation promotes "widespread, systematic disinvestment in the nation's basic productive capacity."[133] Flexible production encourages wage slavery at home. And the search for ever greater profits leads to outsourcing, which accentuates the flight of capital and jobs abroad. Under neoliberalism, the logic of power is articulated through the financial flow of capital and a predatory politics of "accumulation by dispossession through the world in order to keep the motor of accumulation from stalling."[134] Neoliberalism has now become the prevailing logic in the United States, and according to Stanley Aronowitz, "the neoliberal economic doctrine proclaiming the superiority of free markets over public ownership, or even public regulation of private economic activities, has become the conventional wisdom, not only among conservatives but among social progressives."[135] The ideology and power of neoliberalism also cut across national boundaries. Throughout the globe, the forces of neoliberalism are dismantling the historically guaranteed social provisions provided by the welfare state, defining profit-making as the essence of democracy, and equating freedom with the unrestricted ability of markets to "govern economic relations free of government regulation."[136] Transnational in scope, neoliberalism now imposes its economic regime and market values on developing and weaker nations through structural adjustment policies enforced by powerful financial institutions such as the World Bank, the International Monetary Fund (IMF), and the World Trade Organization (WTO). Secure in its dystopian vision that there are no alternatives, as Margaret Thatcher once put it, neoliberalism obviates issues of contingency, struggle, and social agency by promulgating the inevitability of economic laws in which the ethical ideal of intervening in the world gives way to the idea that we "have no choice but to adapt both our hopes and our abilities to the new global market."[137] Coupled with a new culture of fear, market freedoms seem securely grounded in a defense of national security, capital, and property rights.

In its capacity to dehistoricize and depoliticize society, as well as in its aggressive attempts to destroy public spheres necessary for the defense of a genuine democracy, neoliberalism reproduces the conditions for unleashing the most brutalizing forces of capitalism and accentuating the most central elements of proto-fascism. As the late Pierre Bourdieu argued, neoliberalism is a policy of depoliticization, attempting to liberate the economic sphere from all government controls.

> Drawing shamelessly on the lexicon of liberty, liberalism, and deregulation, it aims to grant economic determinisms a fatal stranglehold by liberating them from all controls, and to obtain the submission of citizens and governments to the economic and social forces thus liberated … [T]his policy has imposed itself through the most varied means, especially juridical, on the liberal—or even social democratic-governments of a set of economically advanced countries, leading them gradually to divest themselves of the power to control economic forces.[138]

At the same time, neoliberalism uses the rhetoric of the global victory of free-market rationality to cut public expenditures and undermine those non-commodified public spheres that serve as the repository for critical education, language, and public intervention. Endorsed by the mass media, right-wing intellectuals, and governments alike, neoliberal ideology, with its ongoing emphasis on deregulation and privatization, has found its material expression in an all-out attack on democratic values and on the very notion of the public sphere. Within the discourse of neoliberalism, the notion of the public good is devalued and, where possible, eliminated as part of a wider rationale for a handful of private interests to control as much social life as possible in order to maximize its personal profit. Public services such as health care, child care, public assistance, education, and transportation are now subject to the rules of the market. Construing the public good as a private good and the needs of the corporate and private sector as the only goal of investment, neoliberal ideology produces, legitimates, and exacerbates the existence of persistent poverty, inadequate health care, racial apartheid in the inner cities, and the growing inequalities between the rich and the poor.[139]

As Stanley Aronowitz points out, the Bush administration has made neoliberal ideology the cornerstone of its program, and has been in the forefront in actively supporting and implementing the following policies:

> deregulation of business at all levels of enterprises and trade; tax reduction for wealthy individuals and corporations; the revival of the near-dormant nuclear energy industry; limitations and abrogation of labor's right to organize and bargain collectively; a land policy favoring commercial and industrial development at the expense of conservation and other proenvironment policies; elimination of income support to the chronically unemployed;

reduced federal aid to education and health; privatization of the main federal pension programs, Social Security; limitation on the right of aggrieved individuals to sue employers and corporations who provide services; in addition, as social programs are reduced, [Republicans] are joined by the Democrats in favoring increases in the repressive functions of the state, expressed in the dubious drug wars in the name of fighting crime, more funds for surveillance of ordinary citizens, and the expansion of the federal and local police forces.[140]

Central to neoliberal ideology and its implementation by the Bush administration is the ongoing attempts by free-market fundamentalists and right-wing politicians to view government as the enemy of freedom (except when it aids big business) and to discount it as a guardian of the public interest. The call to eliminate big government is neoliberalism's great unifying idea and has broad popular appeal in the United States because it is a principle deeply embedded in the country's history and tangled up with its notion of political freedom. And yet, the right-wing appropriation of this tradition is racked with contradictions in terms of neoliberal policies. As William Greider points out:

"Leave me alone" is an appealing slogan, but the right regularly violates its own guiding principle. The antiabortion folks intend to use government power to force their own moral values on the private lives of others. Free-market right-wingers fall silent when Bush and congress intrude to bail out airlines, insurance companies, banks—whatever sector finds itself in desperate need. The hard-right conservatives are downright enthusiastic when the

Supreme Court and Bush's Justice Department hack away at our civil liberties. The "school choice" movement seeks not smaller government but a vast expansion of taxpayer obligations.[141]

The advocates of neoliberalism have attacked what they call "big government" when it has provided essential services, such as crucial safety nets for the less fortunate, but they have no qualms about using the government to bail out the airline industry after the economic nose-dive that followed the 2000 election of George W. Bush and the events of 9/11. Nor are there any expressions of outrage from the cheerleaders of neoliberalism when the state engages in promoting various forms of corporate welfare by providing billions of dollars in direct and indirect subsidies to multinational corporations. In short, government bears no obligation for either the poor and dispossessed or the collective future of young people.

As the laws of the market take precedence over the laws of the state as guardians of the public good, the government offers little help in mediating the interface between the advance of capital and its rapacious commercial interests. Nor does it aid non-commodified interests and non-market spheres that create the political, economic, and social spaces and discursive conditions vital for critical citizenship and democratic public life. Within the discourse of neoliberalism, it becomes difficult for the average citizen to speak about political or social transformation, or even to challenge, outside of a grudging nod toward rampant corruption, the ruthless downsizing, the ongoing liquidation of job security, and the elimination of benefits for part-time workers.

AMERICA'S TURN TOWARD AUTHORITARIANISM

The liberal democratic vocabulary of rights, entitlements, social provisions, community, social responsibility, living wage, job security, equality, and justice seems oddly out of place in a country where the promise of democracy has been replaced by casino capitalism, a winner-take-all philosophy, suited to lotto players and day traders alike. As corporate culture extends even deeper into the basic institutions of civil and political society, buttressed daily by a culture industry largely in the hands of concentrated capital, it is reinforced by a pervasive fear and insecurity that the future holds nothing beyond a watered-down version of the present. As the prevailing discourse of neoliberalism seizes the public imagination, there is no vocabulary for progressive social change, democratically inspired visions, or critical notions of social agency to expand the meaning and purpose of democratic public life. Against the reality of low-wage jobs, the erosion of social provisions for a growing number of people, and the expanding war against young people of colour at home, and empire-building abroad, the market-driven juggernaut of neoliberalism continues to mobilize desires in the interest of producing market identities and market relationships that ultimately sever the link between education and social change while reducing agency to the obligations of consumerism.

As neoliberal ideology and corporate culture expand, there is a simultaneous diminishing of non-commodified public spheres—those institutions such as public schools, independent bookstores, churches, noncommercial public broadcasting stations, libraries, trade unions, and various voluntary institutions engaged in dialogue, education, and learning—that address the relationship of the individual to public life, foster social responsibility, and provide a robust vehicle for public participation and democratic citizenship. As media theorists Edward Herman and Robert McChesney observe, non-commodified public spheres have historically played an invaluable role "as places and forums where issues of importance to a political community are discussed and debated, and where information is presented that is essential to citizen participation in community life."[142] Without these critical public spheres, corporate power often goes unchecked and politics becomes dull, cynical, and oppressive.[143] Moreover, in the vacuum left by diminishing democracy, religious zealotry, cultural chauvinism, xenophobia, and racism have become the dominant tropes of neo-conservatives and other extremist groups eager to take advantage of the growing insecurity, fear, and anxiety that result from increased joblessness, the war on terror, and the unraveling of communities. In this context, neo-liberalism creates the instability that helps feed both the neo-conservative and religious Right movements and their proto-fascist policy initiatives.

Especially troubling under the rule of neoliberalism is not just that ideas associated with freedom and agency are defined through the prevailing ideology and principles of the market, but that neoliberal ideology also wraps itself in what appears to be an unassailable appeal to conventional wisdom. Defined as the paragon of modern social relations by Friedrich A. von Hayek, Milton Friedman, Robert Nozick, Francis Fukuyama, and other market fundamentalists, neoliberalism attempts to eliminate any engaged critique about its most basic principles and social consequences by embracing the "market as the arbiter of social destiny."[144] Neoliberalism empties the public treasury, privatizes formerly public services, limits the vocabulary and imagery available to recognize anti-democratic forms of power, and reinforces narrow models of individual agency. Equally important, it undermines the critical functions of a viable democracy by limiting the ability of individuals to engage in the continuous translation between public considerations and private interests, which it accomplishes, in part, by collapsing public issues into the realm of the private. As Bauman observes, "It is no longer true that the 'public' is set on colonizing the 'private'. The opposite is the case: it is the private that colonizes the public space, squeezing out and chasing away everything which cannot be fully, without residue, translated into the vocabulary of private interests and pursuits."[145] Divested of its political possibilities and social underpinnings, freedom offers few opportunities for people to translate private worries into public concerns and collective struggle.[146]

The good life, in this discourse, "is construed in terms of our identities as consumers—we are what we buy."[147] For example, some neoliberal advocates argue that the health care and education crises faced by many states can be solved by selling off public assets to private interests. Blatantly demonstrating neoliberal ideology's contempt for non-commodified public spheres and democratic values, the Pentagon even considered, if only for a short time, turning the war on terror and security concerns over to futures markets, subject to on-line trading. In this exhibition of market logic and casino capitalism, neoliberalism reveals its dream of a social order dominated by commercial spheres. At the same time, it aggressively attempts to empty the substance of critical democracy and replace it with a democracy of goods available to those with purchasing power and the ability to expand the cultural and political power of corporations throughout the world. As a result of the consolidated corporate attack on public life, the maintenance of democratic public spheres from which to launch a moral vision or to engage in a viable struggle over politics loses all credibility—not to mention monetary support. As the alleged objectivity of neoliberal ideology remains largely unchallenged within dominant public spheres, individual critique and collective political struggles become more difficult.[148] This dystopian nightmare gets worse. Dominated by extremists, the Bush administration is driven by an arrogance of power and inflated sense of moral righteousness backed by a false sense of certitude and never-ending posture of triumphalism. George Soros points out that this rigid ideology and inflexible sense of mission allow the Bush administration to believe that "because we are stronger than others, we must know better and we must have right on our side. This is where religious fundamentalism comes together with market fundamentalism to form the ideology of American supremacy."[149]

As public space is commodified and the state becomes aligned with capital, politics is defined by its policing functions rather than as an agency for peace and social reform. Its ideological counterpart is a public pedagogy that mobilizes power in the interest of a social order marked by the progressive removal of autonomous spheres of cultural production such as journalism, publishing, and film; by the destruction of collective structures capable of counteracting the widespread imposition of commercial values and effects of the pure market; by the creation of a global reserve army of the unemployed; and by the subordination of nation-states to the real masters of the economy. Bourdieu emphasizes the effects of neoliberalism on this dystopian world:

> First is the destruction of all the collective institutions capable of counteracting the effects of the infernal machine, primarily those of the state, repository of all of the universal values associated with the idea of the public realm. Second is the imposition everywhere, in the upper spheres of the economy and the state as at the heart of corporations, of that sort of moral Darwinism that, with the cult of the winner, schooled in higher mathematics and bungee jumping, institutes the struggle of all against all and cynicism as the norm of all action and behaviour.[150]

In addition to the destruction of collective solidarities, though never without opposition, neoliberalism refigures the relationship between the state and capital. As the state abandons its social investments in health, education, and the public welfare, it assumes the functions of an enhanced police or security state, the signs of which are most visible in the increasing use of the state apparatus to spy on and arrest its subjects, the incarceration of individuals considered disposable (primarily people of colour), and the ongoing criminalization of social policies. Examples of the latter include anti-begging and anti-loitering ordinances that fine or punish homeless people for sitting or lying down too long in public places.[151] An even more despicable example of the barbaric nature of neoliberalism, with its emphasis on profits over people and its willingness to punish rather than serve the poor and disenfranchised, can be seen in the growing tendency of many hospitals across the country to have patients arrested and jailed if they cannot pay their medical bills. The policy, right out of the pages of George Orwell's *1984*, represents a return to debtors prisons, which is now chillingly called "body attachment," and is "basically a warrant for ... the patient's arrest."[152]

Neoliberalism is not only an economic policy designed to cut government spending, pursue free trade policies, and liberate market forces from government regulations. It is also a political philosophy and ideology that affects every dimension of social life. Neoliberalism has heralded a radical shift that now defines the citizen as a consumer, disbands the social contract in the interests of privatized considerations, and separates capital from the context of place. Within this discourse, as Jean and John Comaroff have argued, "the personal is the only politics there is, the only politics with a tangible referent or emotional valence. It is in these privatized terms that action is organized, that the experience of inequity and antagonism takes meaningful shape."[153] Under such circumstances, neoliberalism portends the death of politics as we know it, strips the social of its democratic values, and reconstructs agency in terms that are utterly privatized. It provides the conditions for an emerging form of proto-fascism that must be resisted at all costs. Neoliberalism not only enshrines unbridled individualism as a central feature of proto-fascism, as Herbert Marcuse reminds us,[154] it also destroys any vestige of democratic society by undercutting its "moral, material, and regulatory moorings,"[155] and, in doing so, offers no language for understanding how the future might be grasped outside the narrow logic of the market. But there is even more at stake here than the obliteration of public concerns, the death of the social, the emergence of a market-based fundamentalism that undercuts our ability to understand how to translate privately experienced misery into collective action, and the elimination of the gains of the welfare state. There is also the growing threat of displacing "political sovereignty with the sovereignty of the market, as if the latter has a mind and morality of its own."[156] As democracy becomes a burden under the reign of neoliberalism, civic discourse disappears and the reign of unfettered social Darwinism, with its survival-of-the-slickest philosophy, emerges as the template for a new form of proto-fascism. None of this will happen in the face of sufficient resistance, nor is the increasing move toward proto-fascism inevitable, but the conditions exist for democracy to lose all semblance of meaning in the United States. Against this encroaching form of fascism, more is needed than moral outrage. What is needed is a new language for theorizing politics in the twenty-first century. Such a language must insist on the fundamental importance of what it means to live in a global information society marked not only by the proliferation of new electronic technologies, but also by new pedagogical sites in which the struggle over meaning is crucial to the realization of the pedagogical conditions necessary for the emergence of democratic modes of agency and collective resistance.[157] Against the increasing alliance among global capitalism, political and religious fundamentalism, and an escalating militarism, there is a need for new social formations in which it becomes possible to imagine a different world, one in which multitudinous networks are joined together not only by a language of critique, but by a language of hope and concerted collective action. Within such a discourse, difference extends into solidarity. Opposition crosses borders and affirms both the collective possibilities of politics and the future as a referent for hope that refuses to stand still.

1   George Monbiot, "Religion of the Rich," *Znet* (November 27, 2004). Available on-line at: http://www.zmag.org/sustainers/content/2004-11/27monbiot.cfm.

2   James Traub, "Weimar Whiners," *New York Times Magazine* (June 1, 2003): 11.

3   David Cole, *No Equal Justice: Race and Class in the American Criminal Justice System* (New York: The New Press, 1999); Christian Parenti, *Lockdown America: Police and Prisons in the Age of Crisis* (London: Verso, 1999); Marc Mauer, *Race to Incarcerate* (New York: The New Press, 1999); Marc Mauer and Meda Chesney-Lind, *Invisible Punishment: The Collateral Consequences of Mass Imprisonment* (New York: The New Press, 2002).

4   Pierre Tristam, "One Man's Clarity in America's Totalitarian Time Warp," *Daytona Beach News-Journal,* January 27, 2004. Available on-line: www.commondreams.org/views0401027-08.htm.

5   Bertram Gross, *Friendly Fascism: The New Face of Power in America* (Montreal: Black Rose Books, 1985).

6   Umberto Eco, "Eternal Fascism: Fourteen Ways of Looking at a Blackshirt," *The New York Review of Books* (November-December 1995), 15.

7   Kevin Passmore, *Fascism* (London: Oxford University Press, 2002), 90.

8   Ibid., 19.

9   Alexander Stille, "The Latest Obscenity Has Seven Letters," *New York Times* (September 13, 2003): 19.

10 Paxton cited in Samantha Power, "The Original Axis of Evil," *The New York Times Book Review* (May 2, 2004). Available on-line: http://query.nytimes.com/gst/fullpage.html?res=9C0CE0DB153AF931A35756C0A9629C8B6. See also Robert O. Paxton, *The Anatomy of Fascism* (New York: Alfred A. Knopf, 2004).

11 Mark Neocleous, *Fascism* (Minneapolis: University of Minnesota Press, 1997), 91.

12 Bill Moyers, "This Is Your Story—The Progressive Story of America. Pass it On," text of speech to the 'Take Back America' Conference (June 4, 2003). Available on-line: www.utoronto.ca/csus/pm/moyers.htm.

13 There has been a drastic increase in income and wealth inequality in the last few decades. For example, Paul Krugman, using data from the Congressional Budget Office, recently showed that "between 1973 and 2000 the average real income of the bottom 90 percent of American taxpayers actually fell by 7 percent. Meanwhile, the income of the top 1 percent rose by 148 percent, the income of the top 0.1 percent rose by 343

percent and the income of the top 0.01 percent rose 599 percent." Paul Krugman, "The Death of Horatio Alger," *The Nation* (January 5, 2004): 16.

14 William Greider, "The Right's Grand Ambition: Rolling Back the 20th Century," *The Nation* (May 12, 2003): 5.

15 See Jürgen Habermas, *The Structural Transformation of the Public Sphere* (1962; Cambridge: MIT Press, 1991); David Harvey, *Spaces of Capital: Towards a Critical Geography* (New York: Routledge, 2001). The literature on the politics of space is far too extensive to cite, but of special interest are Michael Keith and Steve Pile, eds., *Place and the Politics of Identity* (New York: Routledge, 1993); Doreen Massey, *Space, Place, and Gender* (Minneapolis: University of Minnesota, 1994); and Margaret Kohn, *Radical Space: Building the House of the People* (Ithaca: Cornell University Press, 2003).

16 Jo Ellen Green Kaiser, "A Politics of Time and Space," *Tikkun* 18, 6 (2003): 18-19.

17 Margaret Kohn, *Radical Space: Building the House of the People* (Ithaca: Cornell University Press, 2003): 7.

18 Jo Ellen Green Kaiser, 17-18.

19 Zygmunt Bauman, *Globalization: The Human Consequences* (New York: Columbia University Press, 1998): 25-26.

20 Susan Buck-Morss, *Thinking Past Terror* (New York: Verso, 2003): 29.

21 Stanley Aronowitz, *The Last Good Job in America* (Lanham: Rowman and Littlefield, 2001): 160.

22 Richard Falk, "Will the Empire Be Fascist?" *The Transnational Foundation for Peace and Future Research* (March 24, 2003). Available on-line: http://www.transnational.org/forum/meet/2003/Falk_FascistEmpire.html.

23 Victoria de Grazia, *The Culture of Consent: Mass Organization of Leisure in Fascist Italy* (1981; New York: Cambridge University Press, 2002).

24 Eric Alterman, "Pundit Limbo: How Low Can They Go?" *The Nation* (January 31, 2005), 10.

25 Howard Kurts, "Writer Backing Bush Plan Had Gotten Federal Contract," *The Washington Post* (January 26, 2005), C01.

26 David Barstow and Robin Stein, "Under Bush, a New Age of Prepackaged TV News," *The New York Times* (March 31, 2005), 1, 18-19.

27 Eric Alternan, "Bush's War on the Press," *The Nation* (May 9, 2005), 20.

28 Robert McChesney and John Nichols, *Our Media, Not Theirs: The Democratic Struggle*

Against Corporate Media (New York: Seven Stories Press, 2002): 48-49.

29 Jeff Sharlet, "Big World: How Clear Channel Programs America," *Harper's* (December 2003): 38-39.

30 See especially, Mariah Blake, "Stations of the Cross." *Columbia Journalism Review* (May-June, 2005), 1-12.

31 On the relationship between democracy and the media, see Robert W. McChesney, *Rich Media, Poor Democracy: Communication Politics in Dubious Times* (New York: The New Press, 1999).

32 McChesney and Nichols, *Our Media*, 52-53.

33 Transcript of NOW with Bill Moyers, February 13, 2004, 2.

34 Umberto Eco, "Eternal Fascism: Fourteen Ways of Looking at a Blackshirt," *The New York Review of Books* (November-December 1995): 15.

35 Paul O'Neill, former Treasury Secretary who served in the Bush administration for two years, claimed on the January 11, 2004, television program *60 Minutes* that Bush and his advisors started talking about invading Iraq ten days after the inauguration, eight months before the tragic events of September 11th. See CBS News, "Bush Sought Way to Invade Iraq," *60 Minutes* Transcript, July 11th, 2004. Available online: http://www.cbsnews.com/stories/2004/01/09/60minutes/main592330.shtml. For a chronicle of lies coming out of the Bush administration, see David Corn, *The Lies of George Bush* (New York: Crown, 2003).

36 Abbott Gleason, "The Hard Road to Fascism," *Boston Review* (Summer 2003). Available on-line: http://www.bostonreview.net/BR28.3/gleason.html.

37 Bob Herbert, "Casualties at Home," *New York Times,* March 27, 2003, A27.

38 Renana Brooks, "The Language of Power, Fear, and Emptiness," *The Nation* (June 24, 2003). Available on-line: http://reclaimdemocracy.org/weekly-2003/bush-language-power- fear.html.

39 The relevant excerpt from this interview can be found in *Platform Section*, "Millions and Millions Lost," *Harper's* (January 2004), 16.

40 This insight comes from Juan Stam, "Bush's Religious Language," *The Nation* (December 22, 2003), 27.

41 Bush's use of doublespeak is so pronounced that the National Council of Teachers of English awarded him its 2003 Doublespeak Award. See http://www.govst.edu/users/ghrank/Introduction/bush2003.htm.

42 Ruth Rosen, "Bush Doublespeak," *San Francisco Chronicle,* July 14, 2003. Available on-line: www.commondreams.org/views03/0714-10.htm. Also in January 2004, former Vice President Al Gore, in a major speech on Bush's environmental policies, said, "Indeed, they often use Orwellian language to disguise their true purposes. For example, a policy that opens national forests to destructive logging of old-growth trees is labeled Healthy Forest Initiative. A policy that vastly increases the amount of pollution that can be dumped into the air is called the Clear Skies Initiative." Gore cited in Bob Herbert, "Masters of Deception," *The New York Times*, January 16, 2004, A21.

43 Jennifer Lee, "U.S. Proposes Easing Rules on Emissions of Mercury," *The New York Times*, December 3, 2003, A20.

44 Eric Pianin, "Clean Air Rules to Be Relaxed," *The Washington Post* (August 23, 2003). Available on-line: www.washingtonpost.com/ac2/wp-dyn/A34334-2003Aug22?.

45 *The New York Times* reported that the Environmental Protection Agency actually eliminated references to any studies that "concluded that warming is at least partly caused by rising concentrations of smokestack and tail pipe emissions and could threaten health and ecosystems." Cited in Huck Gutman, "On Science, War, and the Prevalence of Lies," *The Statesman* (June 28, 2003). Available on-line: http://www.commondreams.org/views03/0628-04.htm.

46 For all the direct government sources for these lies, see *One Thousand Reasons to Dump George Bush*, especially the section titled "Honesty." Available on-line: http://thousandreasons.org/the_top_ten.html. Also see, David Corn, *The Lies of George W. Bush* (New York: Crown Publishers, 2003).

47 See Corn, *The Lies*, 228-230.

48 The entire Downing Street Memo can be found on-line: www.downingstreetmemo.com.

49 Both quotes are in Paul Krugman, "Standard Operating Procedure," *The New York Times*, June 3, 2004, A17.

50 See Lloyd Grove, "Lowdown," *New York Daily News*, January 11, 2004. The reference is available on-line: www.unknownnews.net/insanity011404.html.

51 Cited in Paul Krugman, "Going for Broke," *The New York Times*, January 20, 2004, A21.

52 Dana Milibank, "Religious Right Finds Its Center in Oval Office," *Washington Post* December 24, 2001, A02.

53 Cited in ibid.

54 Cited in ibid.

55 Cited in Jill Lawrence, "Bush's Agenda Walks the Church-State Line," *USA Today*, January 29, 2003. Available on-line: www.usatoday.com/news/washington/2003-01-29-bush-religion_x.htm.

56 See Stephen Mansfield, *The Faith of George W. Bush* (New York: Tarcher/Penguin, 2003). Cited in Sydney H. Schanberg, "The Widening Crusade," *The Village Voice* October 15-21, 2003. Available on-line: www.villagevoice.com.issues/0342/schanberg.phb.

57 Cited in Bob Herbert, "Stranger than Fiction," *New York Times* (May 9, 2005), A27.

58 Robyn E. Blumner, "Religiosity as Social Policy," *St. Petersburg Times,* September 28, 2003. Available on-line: www.sptimes.com/2003/09/28/news_pf/Columns/religiosity_as_social.shtml.

59 Cited in Paul Harris, "Bush Says God Chose Him to Lead His Nation," *The Guardian*, November 1, 2003. Available on-line: www.observer.co.uk. On the child tax credit, see Bob Herbert, "The Reverse Robin Hood," *The New York Times*, June 2, 2003, A17.

60 Joseph L. Conn, "Faith-Based Fiat," *Americans United for Separation of Church and State* (January 2002). Available on-line: www.au.org/churchstate/cs01031.htm

61 Blumner, "Religiosity as Social Policy."

62 Jonathan Turley, "Raze the Church/State Wall? Heaven Help Us!" *Los Angeles Times*, February 24, 2003. Available on-line: www.enrongate.com/news/index.asp?id=169632.

63 Alan Cooperman, "Paige's Remarks on Religion in Schools Decried," *Washington Post*, April 9, 2003. Available on-line: www.washingtonpost.com/wp-dyn/articles/A59692-2003Apr8.html.

64 Blumner, "Religiosity as Social Policy."

65 Graydon Carter, "The President? Go Figure," *Vanity Fair*, December 2003, 70.

66 John Ashcroft, Remarks to National Religious Broadcasters Convention in Nashville Tennessee on February 19, 2002. Text is distributed by the Department of State and is available on-line: http://usembassy-australia.state.gov/hyper/2002/0219/epf204.htm.

67 Elizabeth Amon, "Name Withheld," *Harper's*, August 2003, 59.

68 Cited in William M. Arkin, "The Pentagon Unleashes a Holy Warrior," *The Los Angeles*

Times, October 16, 2003. Available on-line: www.latimes.com/news/opinion/commentary/la-oe-arkin16oct16,1,2598862,print.st.

69 Arkin, ibid.

70 Cited from transcript from NOW with Bill Moyers, December 26, 2003. Available on-line: http://www.pbs.org/now/transcript/transcript248_full.html.

71 Gary Wills, "With God on His Side," *The New York Times Sunday Magazine* (March 30, 2003), 26.

72 Cited from an interview with Reverend James Forbes, Jr., on NOW with Bill Moyers, December 26, 2003. Available on-line: http://www.pbs.org/now/transcript/transcript248_full.html.

73 "Bill Moyers Interviews Union Theological Seminary's Joseph Hough," NOW with Bill Moyers, October 24, 2003. Available on-line: www.commondreams.org/views03/1027-01.

74 Heather Wokusch, "Make War Not Love: Abstinence, Aggression and the Bush White House," *Common Dreams News Center* (October 23, 2003). Available on-line: www.commondreams.org/views03/1026-01,htm.

75 John R. Gillis, ed., *The Militarization of the Western World* (New Brunswick: Rutgers University Press, 1989). On the militarization of urban space, see Mike Davis, *City of Quartz* (New York: Vintage, 1992); Kenneth Saltman and David Gabbard, eds., *Education as Enforcement: The Militarization and Corporatization of Schools* (New York: Routledge, 2003). For the current neo-conservative influence on militarizing American foreign policy, see Donald Kagen and Gary Schmidt, *Rebuilding America's Defenses* (Sept. 2000), which is one of many reports outlining such an issue, and developed under the auspices of The Project for the New American Century. Available on-line: www.newamericancentury.org.

76 Catherine Lutz, "Making War at Home in the United States: Militarization and the Current Crisis," *American Anthropologist* 104: 723.

77 Kevin Baker, "We're in the Army Now: The G.O.P.'s Plan to Militarize Our Culture," *Harper's* (October 2003), 40.

78 Jorge Mariscal, "'Lethal and Compassionate': The Militarization of US Culture," *CounterPunch* (May 5, 2003). Available on-line http://www.counterpunch.org/mariscal05052003.html.

79 Falk, "Will the Empire be Fascist?" http://www.transnational.org/forum/meet/2003/

Falk_FascistEmpire.html.

80 George Monbiot, "States of War," *The Guardian*, October 14, 2003. Available on-line: www.commondreams.org/views03/1014-09.htm.

81 Mariscal, "'Lethal and Compassionate.'"

82 Baker, "We're in the Army Now."

83 Ibid., 37.

84 Ibid., 37.

85 Ruth Rosen, "Politics of Fear," *The San Francisco Chronicle*, December 30, 2003. Available on-line: www.commondreams.org/views02/1230-02,htm.

86 Fox News's and MSNBC's Iraq war coverage was named by *Time Magazine*, no less, in its "The Year in Culture" section as "the worst display of patriotism" for 2003. See *Time Magazine* (January 5, 2004), 151.

87 Richard H. Kohn, "Using the Military at Home: Yesterday, Today, and Tomorrow," *Chicago Journal of International Law* 94, no.1 (Spring 2003): 174-175.

88 Ibid.

89 David Goodman, "Covertly Recruiting Kids," *The Baltimore Sun,* September 29, 2003. Available on-line: www.commondreams.org/views03/1001-11.htm.

90 Elissa Gootman, "Metal Detectors and Pep Rallies: Spirit Helps Tame a Bronx School," *New York Times*, February 4, 2004, C14.

91 Gail R. Chaddock, "Safe Schools at a Price," *Christian Science Monitor*, August 25, 1999, 15.

92 Tamar Lewin, "Raid at High School Leads to Racial Divide, Not Drugs," *The New York Times*, December 9, 2003, A16.

93 Jeremy Brecher, "Globalization Today" in *Implicating Empire: Globalization & Resistance in the 21st Century World Order*, ed. Stanley Aronowitz & Heather Gautney (New York: Basic Books, 2003), 202.

94 Sara Rimer, "Unruly Students Facing Arrest, Not Detention," *New York Times*, January 2, 2004, 15.

95 Ibid.

96 Randall Beger, "Expansion of Police Power in the Public Schools and the Vanishing Rights of Students," *Social Justice* 29, no.1-2 (2002): 124.

97 Peter B. Kraska, "The Military-Criminal Justice Blur: An Introduction," in *Militarizing the American Criminal Justice System*, ed. Peter B. Kraska (Boston: Northeastern

University Press, 2001), 3.

98 See especially Christian Parenti, *Lockdown America: Police and Prisons in the Age of Crisis* (London: Verso Press, 1999).

99 Kraska, "The Military-Criminal Justice Blur."

100 Jonathan Simon, "Sacrificing Private Ryan: The Military Model and the New Penology," in *Militarizing the American Criminal Justice System*.

101 These figures are taken from the following sources: Gary Delgado, "'Mo' Prisons Equals Mo' Money," *Colorlines* (Winter 1999-2000), 18; Fox Butterfield, "Number in Prison Grows Despite Crime Reduction," *The New York Times*, August 10, 2000, A10.

102 Sanho Tree, "The War at Home," *Sojourner's Magazine* (May-June, 2003), 5.

103 For some extensive analyses of the devastating affects the criminal justice system is having on black males, see Michael Tonry, *Malign Neglect: Race, Crime, and Punishment in America* (New York: Oxford University Press, 1995); Jerome Miller, *Search and Destroy: African-American Males in the Criminal Justice System* (Cambridge: Cambridge University Press, 1996); David Cole, *No Equal Justice: Race and Class in the American Criminal Justice System* (New York: The New Press, 1999); Christian Parenti, *Lockdown America*; Marc Mauer, *Race to Incarcerate* (New York: The New Press, 1999); and Marc Mauer and Meda Chesney-Lind, *Invisible Punishment: The Collateral Consequences of Mass Imprisonment* (New York: The New Press, 2002).

104 Cited in David Barsamian, "Interview with Angela Davis," *The Progressive* (February 2001), 35.

105 Steven Donziger, ed. *The Real War on Crime: The Report of the National Criminal Justice Commission* (New York: Harper, 1996) 101.

106 Lisa Featherstone, "A Common Enemy: Students Fight Private Prisons," *Dissent* (Fall 2000): 78.

107 Carl Chery, "U.S. Army Targets Black Hip-Hop Fans," The Wire/Daily Hip-Hop News, October 21, 2003. Available on-line: *www.sohh.com/article_print.php?content_ID=5162.*

108 Ibid.

109 David Garland cited in Melange, "Men and Jewelry; Prison as Exile; Unifying Laughter and Darkness," *The Chronicle of Higher Education* (July 6, 2001): B4.

110 Mariscal, "Lethal and Compassionate."

111 Matt Slagle, "Military Recruits Video-Game Makers," *Chicago Tribune*, October 8, 2003, 4.

112 Nick Turse, "The Pentagon Invades Your Xbox," *Dissident Voice* (December 15, 2003). Available on-line: www.dissidentvoice.org/Articles9/Turse_Pentagon-Video-Games. htm.

113 For a list of such "toys," see Nicholas Turse, "Have Yourself a Pentagon Xmas," *The Nation*, January 5, 2004, 8. For a more extensive list, visit www.tomdispatch.com.

114 R. Lee Sullivan, "Firefight on Floppy Disk," *Forbes Magazine* (May 20, 1996), 39.

115 Gloria Goodale, "Video Game Offers Young Recruits a Peek at Military Life," *The Christian Science Monitor* (May 31, 2003), 18.

116 Wayne Woolley, "From 'An Army of One' to Army of Fun; Online Video Game Helps Build Ranks," *Times-Picayune*, September 7, 2003, 26.

117 This description comes from *Gaming News* (October 2003) and is available on-line: http://www.gamerstemple.com/news/1003/100331.asp.

118 Ibid.

119 Nick Turse, "The Pentagon Invades Your Xbox," *Dissident Voice* (December 15, 2003). Available on-line: www.dissidentvoice.org/Articles9/Turse_Pentagon-Video-Games. htm.

120 Maureen Tkacik, "Military Toys Spark Conflict on Home Front," *Wall Street Journal*, March 31, 2003, B1.

121 Amy C. Sims, "Just Child's Play," *Fox News* Channel, August 21, 2003. Available on-line: www.wmsa.net/news./Fox News/fn-030822_childs_play.htm.

122 Mike Conklin, "Selling War at Retail," *The Chicago Tribune*, May 1, 2003, 1.

123 Both quotes are from Cathy Horyn, "Macho America Storms Europe's Runways," *The New York Times*, July 3, 2003, A1.

124 Eco, "Eternal Fascism,"13.

125 This quote by Coulter has been cited extensively. It can be found on-line at: http:// www.coulterwatch.com/files/BW_2-003-bin_Coulter.pdf.

126 Baker, "We're in the Army Now," 38.

127 Susan George, "A Short History of Neo-Liberalism: Twenty Years of Elite Economics and Emerging Opportunities for Structural Change," *Global Policy Forum* (March 24-26, 1999). Available on-line: http://www.globalpolicy.org/globaliz/econ/histneol. htm.

128 There are a number of important works on the politics of neoliberalism. I have found the following particularly useful: Pierre Bourdieu, *Acts of Resistance: Against the Tyranny of the Market* (New York: The New Press, 1998); Pierre Bourdieu, "The Essence of Neoliberalism," *Le Monde Diplomatique* (December 1998). On-line at: http://www.en.monde-diplomatique.fr/1998/12/08bourdieu); Zygmunt Bauman, *Work, Consumerism and the New Poor* (London: Polity, 1998); Noam Chomsky, *Profit Over People: Neoliberalism and the Global Order* (New York: Seven Stories Press, 1999); Jean Comaroff and John L. Comaroff, *Millennial Capitalism and the Culture of Neoliberalism* (Durham: Duke University Press, 2000); Anatole Anton, Milton Fisk, and Nancy Holmstrom, eds., *Not for Sale: In Defense of Public Goods* (Boulder: Westview Press, 2000); Alain Touraine, *Beyond Neoliberalism* (London: Polity Press, 2001); Colin Leys, *Market Driven Politics* (London: Verso, 2001); Randy Martin, *Financialization of Daily Life* (Philadelphia: Temple University Press, 2002); Ulrich Beck, *Individualization* (London: Sage, 2002); Doug Henwood, *After the New Economy* (New York: The New Press, 2003); Lisa Duggan, *The Twilight of Equality: Neoliberalism, Cultural Politics, and the Attack on Democracy* (Boston: Beacon Press 2003); and Pierre Bourdieu, *Firing Back: Against the Tyranny of the Market 2*, trans. Loic Wacquant (New York: The New Press, 2003); David Harvey, *The New Imperialism* (New York: Oxford University Press, 2003); Neil Smith, *The Endgame of Globalization* (New York: Routledge, 2005).

129 Minqi Li, "After Neoliberalism," *Monthly Review* (January 2003): 21. Professor Minqi Li provides an important summary of neoliberal polices and their effects. "A neoliberal regime typically includes monetarist policies to lower inflation and maintain fiscal balance (often achieved by reducing public expenditures and raising the interest rate), 'flexible' labor markets (meaning removing labor market regulations and cutting social welfare), trade and financial liberalization, and privatization. These policies are an attack by the global ruling elites (primarily finance capital of the leading capitalist states) on the working people of the world. Under neoliberal capitalism decades of social progress and developmental efforts have been reversed. Global inequality in income and wealth has reached unprecedented levels. In much of the world, working people have suffered pauperization. Entire countries have been reduced to misery (21)."

130 For instance, a United Nations Human Development Report states that "the world's richest 1 percent receive as much income as the poorest 57 percent. The income gap

between the richest 20 percent and the poorest 20 percent in the world rose from 30:1 in 1960 to 60:1 in 1990, and to 74:1 in 1999, and is projected to reach 100:1 in 2015. In 1999-2000, 2.8 billion people lived on less than $3 a day, 840 million were undernourished, 2.4 billion did not have access to any form of improved sanitation services, and one in every six children in the world of primary school age were not in school. About 50 percent of the global nonagricultural labor force is estimated to be either unemployed or underemployed." Cited in Minqi Li, "After Neoliberalism."

131 George Steinmetz, "The State of Emergency and the Revival of American Imperialism; Toward an Authoritarian Post-Fordism," *Public Culture* 15, no.2 (Spring 2003): 337.

132 Ibid.

133 Barry Bluestone and Bennett Harrison, *The Deindustrialization of America: Plant Closings, Community Abandonment and the Dismantling of Basic Industry* (New York: Basic Books, 1982), 6.

134 David Harvey, *The New Imperialism* (New York: Oxford University Press, 2003).

135 Stanley Aronowitz, *How Class Works*, 21.

136 Ibid., 101.

137 Stanley Aronowitz, Introduction to *Pedagogy of Freedom* by Paulo Freire (Lanham: Rowman and Littlefield, 1998), 7

138 Bourdieu, *Firing Back*, 38.

139 See Henwood, *After the New Economy*; Kevin Phillips, *Wealth and Democracy: A Political History of the American Rich* (New York: Broadway, 2003); Paul Krugman, *The Great Unraveling: Losing Our Way in the New Century* (New York: W.W. Norton, 2003).

140 Aronowitz, *How Class Works,* 102.

141 William Greider, "The Right's Grand Ambition: Rolling Back the 20th Century," *The Nation*, May 12, 2003, 8.

142 Edward S. Herman and Robert W. McChesney, *The Global Media: The New Missionaries of Global Capitalism* (Washington and London: Cassell, 1997), 3.

143 I address this issue in Henry A. Giroux, *Public Spaces, Private Lives: Democracy Beyond 9/11* (Lanham: Rowman and Littlefield, 2003).

144 James Rule, "Markets, in Their Place," *Dissent* (Winter 1998): 31.

145 Zygmunt Bauman, *The Individualized Society* (London: Polity Press, 2001): 107.

146 Ibid.

147 Alan Bryman, *Disney and His Worlds* (New York: Routledge, 1995): 154.

148 Of course, there is widespread resistance to neoliberalism and its institutional enforcers, such as the WTO and IMF, among many intellectuals, students, and global justice movements, but this resistance rarely gets aired in the dominant media and, if it does, it is often dismissed as irrelevant or tainted by Marxist ideology.

149 George Soros, "The US Is Now in the Hands of a Group of Extremists," *The Guardian*, January 26, 2004. Available on-line: www.commondreams.org/views04/0126-01.htm.

150 Pierre Bourdieu, "The Essence of Neoliberalism," *Le Monde Diplomatique* (December 1998), 4. Available on-line: http://www.en.monde-diplomatique.fr/1998/12/08bourdieu).

151 Paul Tolme, "Criminalizing the Homeless," *In These Times* (April 14, 2003), 6-7.

152 Staff of *Democracy Now*, "Uncharitable Care: How Hospitals are Gouging and Even Arresting the Uninsured," *Common Dreams* (January 8, 2004). Available on-line: http://www.commondreams.org/headlines04/0108-07.htm.

153 John and Jean Comaroff, "Millennial Capitalism: First Thoughts on a Second Coming," *Public Culture*, 12:2 (2000): 305.

154 Herbert Marcuse, *Technology, War and Fascism: The Collected Papers of Herbert Marcuse*, volume I, ed. Douglas Kellner (New York: Routledge, 1998).

155 John and Jean Comaroff, "Millennial Capitalism," 332.

156 Ibid.

157 See Scott Lash, *Critique of Information* (Thousand Oaks, CA: Sage, 2002).

2

EDUCATION AFTER ABU GHRAIB: REVISITING ADORNO'S POLITICS OF EDUCATION[1]

"The gulag of our time."   —Amnesty International (2005)

"Every image of the past that is not recognized by the present as one of its own concerns threatens to disappear irretrievably."
                                        —Walter Benjamin

Warring Images

Visual representations of the war in Iraq have played a prominent role in shaping public perceptions of the United States's invasion and occupation. The initial, much-celebrated, image widely used to represent the war captured the toppling of the statue of Saddam Hussein in Baghdad soon after the invasion. The second image, also one of high drama and spectacle, portrayed President Bush in full flight gear after his "Top Gun" landing on the deck of the *USS Abraham Lincoln*. The scripted photo-op included a banner behind the President proclaiming "Mission Accomplished."

The mainstream media gladly seized upon the first image. It reinforced the presuppositions that the invasion was a justified response to the hyped-up threat of Saddam's regime and that his fall was the outcome of an extension of American democracy and an affirmation of America's role as a beneficent empire, animated by "the use of military power to shape the world according to American interests and values."[2] The second image fed into the scripted representations of Bush as a "tough," even virile, leader who had taken on the garb of a Hollywood warrior determined to protect the United States from terrorists and to bring the war in Iraq to a quick and successful conclusion.[3] The narrow ideological field that framed these images in the American media proved impervious to dissenting views, exhibiting a disregard for accurate or critical reporting, as well as indifference to fulfilling the media's traditional role as a fourth estate, as guardians of democracy and defenders of the public interest. Slavishly reporting the war as if they were on the Pentagon payroll, the dominant media rarely called into question the Bush administration's reasons for going to war or the impact the war was to have on the Iraqi people and on US domestic and foreign policy.

In the spring of 2004, a new set of images challenged the mythic representations of the Iraqi invasion with the release of hundreds of gruesome photographs and videos documenting the torture of Iraqi prisoners by American soldiers at Abu Ghraib. They were first broadcast on the television series *60 Minutes II* and later leaked to the press, becoming something of a nightly feature in the weeks and months that ensued. Abu Ghraib prison was one of the most notorious sites used by the deposed Hussein regime to inflict unspeakable horrors on those Iraqis considered disposable for various political reasons. Ironically, the photos reinforced the growing perception in the Arab world that one tyrant simply had replaced another. In sharp contrast to the all-too-familiar and officially sanctioned images of good-hearted and stalwart US soldiers patrolling dangerous Iraqi neighbourhoods, caring for wounded soldiers, or passing out candy to young Iraqi children, the newly discovered photos depicted Iraqi detainees being humiliated and tortured. The face of the US invasion was soon recast by a number of sadistic images, including now-infamous photos depicting the insipid, grinning faces of Specialist Charles A. Graner and Pfc. Lynndie R. England flashing a thumbs-up behind a pyramid of seven naked detainees, a kneeling inmate posing as if he is performing oral sex on another hooded male detainee, a terrified male Iraqi inmate trying to ward off an attack dog being handled by US soldiers, and a US soldier grinning next to the body of a dead inmate packed in ice. Two of the most haunting images depicted a hooded man standing on a box with his arms outstretched in Christ-like fashion, electric wires attached to his hands and penis. Another image revealed a smiling L.R. England holding a leash attached to a naked Iraqi man lying on the floor of the prison. Like Oscar Wilde's infamous picture of Dorian Gray, the portrait of American democracy was irrevocably transformed into its opposite. The fight for Iraqi hearts and minds was now irreparably damaged as the war on terror appeared to produce only more terror, mimicking the very crimes it claimed to have eliminated.

As Susan Sontag points out, the leaked photographs include both the victims and their gloating assailants. For Sontag, the images from Abu Ghraib are not only "representative of the fundamental corruptions of any foreign occupation and its distinctive policies which serve as a perfect recipe for the cruelties and crimes in American run prisons.... [but are also] like lynching pictures and are treated as souvenirs of a collective action."[4] Reminiscent of photos taken by whites who lynched blacks after Reconstruction, the images were circulated as trophy shots to be passed around and sent out to friends. For Sontag and others, Abu Ghraib could not be understood outside the racism and brutality that accompanied the exercise of nearly unchecked, unaccountable, absolute power at home and abroad. Similarly, Sidney Blumenthal argues that Abu Ghraib was a predictable consequence of the Bush administration's policy to fight terrorism by creating a system "beyond law to defend the rule of law against terrorism." One consequence of such obscenely ironic posturing, as he points out, is a Gulag,

> that stretches from prisons in Afghanistan to Iraq, from Guantanamo to secret CIA prisons around the world. There are perhaps 10,000 people being held in Iraq, 1,000 in Afghanistan and almost 700 in Guantanamo, but no one knows the exact numbers. The law as it applies to them is whatever the executive deems necessary. There has been nothing like this system since the fall of the Soviet Union.[5]

As time passed, it became clear that the instances of abuse and torture at Abu Ghraib were extensive, systemic, and part of a larger pattern of criminal behaviour that had taken place in other prisons in both Iraq and Afghanistan—not to mention the prisons on the home front.[6] Patterns of mistreatment by US soldiers had also taken place in Camp Bucca, a US-run detention centre in southern Iraq, as well as in an overseas CIA interrogation centre at the Bagram air base in Afghanistan, where the deaths of three detainees were labelled as homicides by US military doctors.[7]

The most compelling evidence refuting the argument that what happened at Abu Ghraib was the result of the actions of a few isolated individuals who strayed from protocol is spelled out by Seymour Hersh in his May 10, 2004, *New Yorker* article, in which he analyzes the fifty-eight-page classified report by Major General Antonio Taguba, who investigated the abuses at Abu Ghraib. In the report, Taguba insisted that "a huge leadership failure"[8] at Abu Ghraib was responsible for what he described as "sadistic, blatant, and wanton criminal abuses."[9] Taguba not only documented examples of torture and sexual humiliation; he also elaborated on the range of indignities, which included:

> Breaking chemical lights and pouring the phosphoric liquid on detainees; pouring cold water on naked detainees; beating detainees with a broom handle and a chair; threatening male detainees with rape; allowing a military police guard to stitch the wound of a detainee who was injured after being slammed against the wall in his cell; sodomizing a detainee with a chemical light and perhaps a broomstick, and using military working dogs to frighten and intimidate detainees with threats of attack, and in one instance actually biting a detainee.[10]

Taguba's report reveals scenes of abuse more systemic than aberrant, but also tragically familiar to communities of colour on the domestic front, long subjected to profiling, harassment, intimidation, and brutality by law-and-order professionals.

The Politics of Delay and Outrage

Responses from around the world exhibited outrage and disgust over the US actions at Abu Ghraib. The rhetoric of American democracy was denounced all over the globe as hypocritical and utterly propagandistic, especially in light of President Bush's April 30, 2004, remarks claiming that with the removal of Saddam Hussein, "there are no longer torture chambers or mass graves or rape rooms in Iraq."[11] The protracted release of new sets of pictures of US soldiers grinning as they tortured and sexually humiliated Iraqi prisoners at Abu Ghraib further undermined the moral and political credibility of the United States both in the Arab world and around the globe. Restoring one of Saddam Hussein's most infamous torture chambers to its original use reinforced the image of the United States as a dangerous, rogue state with despicable imperial ambitions. As columnist Katha Pollitt puts it,

> The pictures and stories [from Abu Ghraib] have naturally caused a furor around the world. Not only are they grotesque in themselves, they reinforce the pre-existing impression of Americans as racist, cruel and frivolous. They are bound to alienate—further alienate—Iraqis who hoped that the invasion would lead to secular democracy and a normal life and who fear Islamic rule. Abroad, if not here at home, they underscore how stupid and wrong the invasion of Iraq was in the first place, how predictably

the 'war of choice' that was going to be a cakewalk has become a brutal and corrupt occupation, justified by a doctrine of American exceptionalism that nobody but Americans believes.[12]

But Abu Ghraib did more than inspire moral revulsion. It also became a rallying cry for recruiting radical extremists as well as producing legitimate opposition to the American occupation. At one level, the image of the faceless, hooded detainee, arms outstretched and wired, conjured images of the Spanish Inquisition, the French brutalization of Algerians, and the slaughter of innocent people at My Lai during the Vietnam war. The heavily damaged rhetoric of American democracy now gave way to the more realistic discourse of empire, colonization, and militarization. At another level, the images shed critical light on the frequently ignored connection between US domination abroad, often aimed at the poor and dispossessed, and at home, particularly against people of colour, including the lynching of American blacks in the first half of the twentieth century and the increasingly brutalizing incarceration of large numbers of youth of colour that continues into the new millennium. Patricia Williams links the criminal abuse of Iraqi detainees at Abu Ghraib prison to a web of secrecy, violation of civil rights, and racist violence that has become commonplace on the domestic front. She writes:

> [I]t's awfully hard not to look at those hoods and think Inquisition; or the piles of naked and sodomized men and think Abner Louima; or the battered corpses and think of Emmett Till. ... This mess is the predictable byproduct of any authority that starts "sweeping" up "bad guys" and holding them without

charge, in solitary and in secret, and presuming them guilty. It flourished beyond the reach of any formal oversight by Congress, by lawyers or by the judiciary, a condition vaguely rationalized as "consistent with" if not "precisely" pursuant to the Geneva Conventions. Bloodied prisoners were moved around to avoid oversight by international observers, a rather too disciplined bit of sanitizing.[13]

Outrage abroad was matched by often low-keyed, if not crude, responses by those implicated, whether in military barracks or Washington offices. For the high priests of "personal responsibility," it was a study in passing the buck. President Bush responded by claiming that what happened at Abu Ghraib was nothing more than "disgraceful conduct by a few American troops."[14] General Richard Myers, chairman of the Joint Chiefs of Staff, suggested it was the work of a "handful" of enlisted individuals.[15] But the claim that the Pentagon was unaware of the Abu Ghraib was at odds not only with International Red Cross reports that regularly notified the Pentagon of such crimes. It was further contradicted by the Taguba report as well as by a series of memos leaked to the press, indicating that the White House, Pentagon, and Justice Department had attempted to justify interrogation practices that violated the federal anti-torture statute two years prior to the invasion.

One such memo was written in August 2002 by Assistant Attorney General Jay S. Bybee, head of the Justice Department's Office of Legal Counsel. He argued that in a post-9/11 world, any attempt to apply the Geneva Convention Against Torture undermined presidential power and should be considered unconstitutional. More specifically, the Bybee memo argued "on behalf of the Justice Department that the President could order the use of torture."[16] Attorney General Alberto Gonzales, then a high-ranking government lawyer, argued in a draft memo to President Bush on January 25, 2002, that the Geneva Conventions are "quaint," if not "obsolete," and that certain forms of traditionally unauthorized methods of inflicting physical and psychological pain might be justified under the aegis of fighting the war on terrorism.[17] In commenting on the memo, Anthony Lewis states, "Does he believe that any treaty can be dismissed when it is inconvenient to an American government?"[18] In fact, confidential legal memoranda produced by the Justice Department flatly stated that the "administration is not bound by prohibitions against torture."[19] A Defense Department memo echoed the same line in a calculated attempt to incorporate torture as part of normal interrogating procedures in defiance of international protocols. The *Wall Street Journal* reported on June 7, 2004, that these memos "sought to assign the President virtually unlimited authority on matters of torture."[20] Exercising rhetorical licence in defining torture in narrow terms, they ended up legitimizing interrogation practices at odds with both the Geneva Conventions and the army's own *Field Manual* for intelligence, which prohibits "the use of force, mental torture, threats, insults or exposure to unpleasant and inhumane treatment of any kind."[21] In reviewing the government's case for torture, Anthony Lewis writes:

> The memos read like the advice of a mob lawyer to a mafia don
> on how to skirt the law and stay out of prison. Avoiding pros-

> ecution is literally a theme of the memoranda. ... Another theme
> in the memoranda, an even more deeply disturbing one, is that
> the President can order the torture of prisoners even though it is
> forbidden by a federal statute and by the International Conven-
> tion Against Torture, to which the United States is a party. ... the
> issues raised by the Bush administration's legal assertions in its
> "war on terror" are so numerous and so troubling that one hardly
> knows where to begin discussing them. The torture and death of
> prisoners, the end result of cool legal abstractions, have a power-
> ful claim on our national conscience. ... But equally disturbing,
> in its way, is the administration's constitutional argument that
> presidential power is unconstrained by law.[22]

Both then-Attorney General John Ashcroft and Secretary of Defense
Donald Rumsfeld denied any involvement by the Bush administration
in providing the legal sanctions for torture or for creating the conditions
that made the abuses at Abu Ghraib possible. Ashcroft refused the Senate Judiciary Committee's request to make public a 2002 Justice Department memo sanctioning high-risk interrogation tactics that may violate
the federal anti-torture statute, while he repeatedly insisted that the Bush
administration does not sanction torture. When the Abu Ghraib scandal
first broke in the press and reporters asked him about the Taguba report,
Rumsfeld claimed he hadn't read it.

When reporters raised questions about Seymour Hersh's charge
that Rumsfeld had personally approved a clandestine program known as
SAP, "that encouraged physical coercion and sexual humiliation of Iraqi
prisoners in an effort to generate more intelligence about the growing in-

surgency in Iraq," Pentagon spokesman Lawrence Di Rita responded by calling Hersh's article "outlandish, conspiratorial, and filled with error and anonymous conjecture."[23] At the same time, Di Rita did not directly rebut any of Hersh's claims. When confronted directly about the charge that he authorized a secret program that was given the blanket approval to kill, torture, and interrogate high-value targets, Rumsfeld performed a semantic tap dance that would have made Bill Clinton blush. He told reporters: "My impression is that what has been charged thus far is abuse, which I believe technically is different from torture…I don't know if…it is correct to say what you just said, that torture has taken place, or that there's been a conviction for torture. And therefore I am not going to address the torture word."[24] But Rumsfeld's contempt for the Geneva Conventions and established military protocol was made public soon after the war on terror was launched in 2001. Disdaining a military machine shaped by the "old rules," he believed they prevented the military and its leadership from taking "greater risks."[25] In 2002, he went so far as to claim that "complaints about America's treatment of prisoners…amounted to 'isolated pockets of international hyperventilation.'"[26] It was later revealed in at least two reports and a range of news sources, including the *Wall Street Journal* and *Newsweek*, that Rumsfeld had indeed supported interrogation techniques against the Taliban and Iraqi prisoners that violated the Geneva Conventions. As the facts surrounding the abuses emerged belatedly in the dominant media, he admitted he was responsible for the hiding of "Ghost detainees" from the Red Cross and asserted before a Senate Committee that he would assume the blame for Abu Ghraib, but also refused to resign, though he later said on the *Larry King Show* that he had submitted his resignation twice after the Abu Ghraib scandal and the president refused to accept it.

What became clear soon after the scandal of Abu Ghraib went public was that it could not be reduced to the "failure of character" of a few soldiers, as George W. Bush insisted. Nor could it be seen as behaviour entirely antithetical to the values and practices of American democracy. In June 2004, the *New York Times* and the *Washington Post* broke even more stories documenting the use of torture-like practices by US soldiers who subjected prisoners to unmuzzled military dogs as part of a contest waged to see how many detainees they could make involuntarily urinate out of fear of the dogs,[27] and who forced detainees to stand on boxes and sing "The Star Spangled Banner" in the nude. Both tactics took place long before the famous photographs were taken at Abu Ghraib.[28] Far from the "frat boy pranks" to which apologists compared the torture, these acts were designed to inflict maximal damage—performed on detainees whose culture views nudity as a violation of religious principles and associates public nudity with shame and guilt. Equally disturbing is the International Committee of the Red Cross estimate that 70 to 90 percent of the detainees arrested by coalition troops "had been arrested by mistake" and had nothing to do with terrorism.[29] It gets worse. Since the release of the initial photos, a new round of fresh photographs and film footage of torture from Abu Ghraib and other prisons in Iraq "include details of the rape and ... abuse of some of the Iraqi women and the hundred or so children—some as young as 10 years old."[30] One account provided by US Army Sargent Samuel Provance, who was stationed in the Abu Ghraib prison, recalls "how interrogators soaked a 16-year-old, covered him in mud, and then used his suffering to break the youth's father, also a prisoner, during interrogation."[31] An army investigation also revealed that unmuzzled military police dogs were employed at Abu Ghraib prison as part of a sadistic game used to "make juveniles—as young as 15 years old—urinate on themselves as part of a competition."[32] Recent reports in the press indicate that prostitutes and female interrogators "used a toxic combination of sex and religion" to taunt and abuse prisoners not only in Abu Ghraib, but also in the US prison camp in Cuba.[33] In some instances, female interrogators sexually fondled inmates, spread fake menstrual blood on them, and paraded in front of them wearing tight tee-shirts and thong underwear. One prisoner, Mamdouh Habib, said he had been subjected to atrocities fit for "a vulgar concentration camp." He told his lawyer that "a prostitute stood over him naked while he was strapped to the floor and menstruated on him."[34]

The wanton abuse of Iraqi detainees, including women and children,[35] the ongoing efforts at the highest levels of the Bush administration to establish new legal ground for torture, and the use of private contractors to perform the dirty work of interrogating detainees in order to skirt what is clearly an abdication of civil and military law are evidence of a systemic, widespread collusion with crimes against humanity. In spite of claims by the Bush administration that such abuses are the work of a few rogue soldiers, inquiries by high-level outside panels, especially the four-member

Schlesinger panel, have concluded that the Abu Ghraib abuses point to leadership failures at the "highest levels of the Pentagon, Joint Chiefs of Staff and military command in Iraq."[36] Such reports and the increasing revelations of the extent of the abuse and torture perpetuated in Iraq, Afghanistan, and American prisons do more than promote moral outrage at the growing injustices practised by the US government. They also position the United States as one more rogue regime sharing, as an editorial in the *Washington Post* pointed out, the company of former military juntas "in Argentina and Chile... that claim[ed] torture is justified when used to combat terrorism."[37] More recently, a Pentagon report headed by Vice Admiral Albert T. Church III of the navy increased the number of detainees murdered by American troops and government personnel in Iraq to twenty-six, but at the same time refused to assign blame to senior defense department civilians and military commanders and concluded that "the abuse of prisoners in Iraq and Afghanistan had been the result primarily of a breakdown in discipline, not flawed policies or misguided direction from commanders or Pentagon officials."[38] Church's report does more than contradict the Schlesinger report. It adds fuel to the call by many politicians and human rights groups that an independent inquiry be established both to examine the full range of detainee abuse and torture in Iraq and Afghanistan and to determine the accountability of senior leaders in such crimes. For example, James D. Ross, senior legal advisor for Human Rights Watch in New York argued that "This [report] just reflects an overall failure to take seriously the abuses that have occurred."[39] The call for an independent inquiry appears more urgent in light of a recent high-level Army investigation clearing four of the five top Army officers at Abu Ghraib prison of any responsibility for the abuse and torture of detainees under their control.[40] The message is clear. Abu Ghraib was an aberration of low-level soldier incompetence rather than a symptom of war crimes perpetrated at the highest levels of government and military power. Or as Fay Bowers puts it, "the lowest level soldier has the highest level of responsibility." [41]

In spite of the extensive photographic proof, international and internal reports, and journalistic accounts revealing egregious brutality, racism, and inhumanity by American soldiers against Arab detainees, conservative pundits took their cue from the White House, attempting to justify such detestable acts and defend the Bush administration's usurpation of presidential power. Powerful right-wing ideologues such as Rush Limbaugh and Cal Thomas defended such actions as simply a way for "young men" to "blow off some steam," engage in forms of harmless frat hazing, or give Muslim prisoners what they deserve. More offensive than the blasé attitudes of talking heads was the mantle of moral authority and outrage assumed by politicians who took umbrage with those who dared criticize Bush or his army at a time of war. Former Speaker of the House Newt Gingrich and Republican Senator James Inhofe insisted that calling attention to such crimes not only undermined troop morale in Iraq, but was also deeply unpatriotic. Inhofe actually stated publicly at a Senate Armed Services Committee hearing that he was outraged by the "outrage everyone seems to have about the treatment of these prisoners. ... I am also outraged by the press and the politicians and the political agendas that are being served by this.... I am also outraged that we have so many humanitarian do-gooders right now crawling all over these prisons looking for human rights violations while our troops, our heroes, are fighting and dying."[42] That many of these prisoners were innocent civilians picked up in indiscriminate sweeps by the US military, or that US troops were operating a chamber of horrors at Abu Ghraib, was irrelevant, providing fodder for silencing criticism by labelling it unpatriotic, or for scapegoating the "liberal" media for reporting such injustices. Inhofe represents a prime example of how politics is corrupted by a dangerous ethos of divine right informed by the mythos of American exceptionalism and a patriotic fervour that disdains reasonable dissent and moral critique. Inhofe's arrogant puffery must be challenged, not only for shutting down dialogue, but also for the egregious way in which it invites Americans to identify with the violence of the torturers. What are we to make of a society that issues public statements condoning torture, especially when these statements are made by powerful politicians?

Other conservatives such as Watergate-felon-turned-preacher Charles Colson, Robert Knight of the Culture and Family Institute, and Rebecca Hagelin, the vice-president of the Heritage Foundation, assumed the moral high ground, blaming what happened at Abu Ghraib on the debauchery of popular culture. Invoking the tired language of the culture wars, Colson argued that "the prison guards had been corrupted by a 'steady diet of MTV and pornography.'" Knight argued that the depravity exhibited at Abu Ghraib was modelled after gay porn that gave military personnel "the idea to engage in sadomasochistic activity and to video-tape in voyeuristic fashion." Rebecca Hagelin viewed the prison scandal as the outcome of a general moral laxity in which "our country permits Hollywood to put almost anything in a movie and still call it PG-13."[43] For those hard-wired Bush supporters who wanted to do more than blame Hollywood porn, MTV, prime-time television, and (not least) gay culture, the scandalous images themselves were seen as the source of the problem because of the offensive nature of their representations and the controversy they generated.

Despite the colossal (and it seems deliberate) misrepresentations of the facts leading to the war with Iraq, along with the neo-conservative and Christian fundamentalism driving the Bush presidency and its disastrous policies at home and abroad, Bush's credibility remains intact for many conservatives. Consequently, they ignore the underlying conditions that gave rise to the horrific abuses at Abu Ghraib, removing them from the inventory of unethical and damaging practices associated with American exceptionalism and triumphalism. Thus, they ignore Bush's disastrous, open-ended war on terrorism and how it has failed to protect the American populace at home, while sanctioning wars abroad used as recruiting tools for Islamic terrorists; Bush's doctrine of secrecy[44] and unaccountability; Bush's suspension of basic civil liberties under the USA PATRIOT Act and his willingness to include some named terrorists under the designation of enemy combatants so as to remove them from the protection of the law;

and the Bush administration's all-out assault on the social contract and the welfare state.[45] Treating the Bush presidency as sacrosanct—and so, unaccountable and beyond public engagement—enables conservatives to conveniently overlook their own complicity in furthering those existing relations of power and politics that make the dehumanizing events of Abu Ghraib possible. Within this apologetic discourse, matters of individual and collective responsibility disappear in a welter of hypocritical and strategic diversions. As *New York Times* columnist Frank Rich puts it,

> the point of these scolds' political strategy—and it is a political strategy, despite some of its adherents' quasireligiosity—is clear enough. It is not merely to demonize gays and the usual rogue's gallery of secularist bogeymen for any American ill but to clear the Bush administration of any culpability for Abu Ghraib, the disaster that may have destroyed its mission in Iraq. If porn or MTV or Howard Stern can be said to have induced a "few bad apples" in one prison to misbehave, then everyone else in the chain of command, from the commander-in-chief down, is off the hook. If the culture war can be cross-wired with the actual war, then the buck will stop not at the Pentagon or the White House but at the Paris Hilton video, or *Mean Girls*, or maybe *Queer Eye for the Straight Guy*.[46]

When it comes to reconciling barbarous acts of torture and humiliation with the disingenuous rhetoric of democracy so popular among conservatives, the issue of blame can assume a brutalizing character. For instance, several conservatives (as well as those responsible for the September 11, 2004, report by the army's Inspector General and a 2005 high-level Army investigation) place the causes for abuse at Abu Ghraib at the doorstep of low-ranking personnel who, once considered disposable fodder for the war effort, now provide equally talented scapegoats. Powerless to defend themselves against the implied accusation that their working-class and rural backgrounds produced the propensity for sexual deviancy and cruelty in the grand style of the film *Deliverance*, they merely claimed to be following orders. But class hatred proved a serviceable means to deflect attention from the Bush administration. How else to explain Republican Senator Ben Campbell's comment that "I don't know how these people got into our army"?[47] But class antagonism was not the only weapon in right-wing arsenals. Even more desperate, Ann Coulter blames Abu Ghraib on the allegedly aberrant nature of women, particularly evident in her assertion that "This is yet another lesson in why women shouldn't be in the military. . . . Women are more vicious than men."[48] All these arguments, as Rich points out, share in an effort to divert attention from matters of politics and history in order to clear the Bush administration of any wrongdoing.[49] Of course, I am not suggesting that Lynndie England, Sabrina Harman, Jeremy Sivits, Charles Graner, Jr., and others should not be held responsible for their actions. In fact, many of them have been found guilty by military courts. Rather, my claim is that responsibility for Abu Ghraib does not lie with them alone. And, yet, as recent reports by the American Civil Liberties Union and the International Committee of the Red Cross make clear, the torture and abuse inflicted by American soldiers and private contractors were not limited to Abu Ghraib, taking place throughout Iraq,

Afghanistan, and in Camp Delta, Cuba. Still President Bush has not only refused to acknowledge responsibility for the scope and gravity of such acts, but has actually rewarded those officials in the highest levels of government responsible for the torture, even as the military scapegoats low-ranking personnel. For instance, Alberto R. Gonzales, who wrote the memos paving the way for validating torture and dismissing the Geneva Conventions, has now been appointed as Attorney General; Donald Rumsfeld has been rewarded with a second term appointment as Secretary of Defense; and Jay S. Bybee, "who wrote a legal opinion on maximizing the kind of brutal treatment that the United States could legally defend," was "subsequently rewarded with a nomination to a federal Court of Appeals."[50]

Abu Ghraib Photographs and the Politics of Public Pedagogy

Susan Sontag has argued that photographs lay down the "tracks for how important conflicts are judged and remembered."[51] But, at the same time, she makes it very clear that all photographs cannot be understood through one language recognized by all. Photographs are never transparent, existing outside of the "taint of artistry or ideology."[52] Understood as social and historical constructs, photographic images entail acts of translation necessary to mobilize compassion instead of indifference, witnessing rather than consuming, and critical engagement rather than aesthetic appreciation or crude repudiation. Put differently, photographs such as those that revealed the horrors at Abu Ghraib prison have no guaranteed meaning, but, rather, exist within a complex of shifting mediations that are material,

128

historical, social, ideological, and psychological in nature.[53]

Hence, the photographic images from Abu Ghraib prison cannot be interpreted outside history, politics, or ideology. This is not to suggest that photographs do not record some element of reality. However, what they capture can only be understood as part of a broader engagement with cultural politics and its intersection with various dynamics of power, all of which inform the conditions for reading photographs as both a pedagogical intervention and a form of cultural production.[54] Photographic images do not reside in the unique vision of their producer or in the reality they attempt to capture. Representations privilege those who have some control over self-representation, and they are largely framed within dominant modes of intelligibility.

The Abu Ghraib photographs are constitutive of diverse sites and technologies of pedagogy, and, as such, represent political and ethical forms of address that make moral demands and claims upon their viewers. Questions of power and meaning are always central to any discussion of photographic images. Such images not only register the cultural mythologies that must be critically mediated; they also represent ideological modes of address tied to the limits of human discourse and intelligibility, and function as pedagogical practices regarding how agency should be organized and represented. The pictures of abuse at Abu Ghraib prison gain their status as a form of public pedagogy by virtue of the spaces they create between the sites in which they become public and the forms of pedagogical address that both frame and mediate their meaning. As they circulate through various sites, including talk radio, computer screens, television, newspapers, the Internet, and alternative media, they initiate different forms of address, mobilize different cultural meanings, and offer different sites of learning. The meanings that frame the images from Abu Ghraib prison are "contingent upon the pedagogical sites in which they are considered"[55] and which limit or rule out certain questions, historical inquiries, and explanations. For example, news programs on the Fox television network systematically occlude any criticism of the images of abuse at Abu Ghraib that would call into question the American presence in Iraq. If such issues are raised, they are dismissed as unpatriotic.

Attempts to defuse or rewrite images that treat people as things, as less than human, have a long history. Commentators have invoked comparisons to the images of the lynchings of black men and women in the American south and Jews in Nazi death camps.[56] John Louis Lucaites and James P. McDaniel have documented how *Life Magazine*, during World War II, put a photograph on its cover of a woman gazing pensively at the skull of a Japanese soldier sent to her by her boyfriend serving in the Pacific, a lieutenant who, when he left to fight in the war "promised her a Jap."[57] Far from reminding its readers of the barbarity of war, the magazine invoked the patriotic gaze in order to frame the barbaric image as part of a public ritual of mortification and a visual marker of humiliation.

As forms of public pedagogy, photographic images must be engaged ethically as well as socio-politically because they are implicated in history and they frequently work to suppress the very conditions that produce them. Often framed within dominant forms of circulation and meaning, such images generally legitimate particular forms of recognition and meaning marked by diversion and evasion. This position is evident in those politicians who believe that the photographs from Abu Ghraib are the real problem, rather than the conditions that produced them; or in the endless commentaries that view the abuses at Abu Ghraib as caused by a few "bad apples." Subjecting such public pronouncements to critical inquiry can only occur within those pedagogical sites and practices in which matters of critique and a culture of questioning are requisite to a vibrant and functioning democracy. But public pedagogy at its best offers more than forms of reading that are critical and relate cultural texts, such as photographs, to the larger world. Public pedagogy defines the cultural objects of interpretation, and offers the possibility for engaging modes of literacy that are not just about competency, but also about the possibility of interpretation as an intervention in the world. While it is true, as Arthur C. Danto insists, that images such as those associated with Abu Ghraib "tell us something worth knowing about where we are as a culture,"[58] meaning does not rest with the images alone, but with the ways in which they are aligned and shaped by larger institutional and cultural discourses, and how they call into play the condemnation of torture (or its celebration), how it came about, and what it means to prevent it from happening again. This is a pedagogical and a political issue. Making the political more pedagogical in this instance connects what we know to the conditions that make learning possible in the first place. It creates opportunities to be critical, but also, as Judith Butler notes, to "take stock of our world, and [participate] in its social transformation in such a way that non-violent, cooperative, egalitarian international relations remain the guiding ideal."[59] While Sontag and others are quite perceptive in pointing to the political nature of reading images, a politics concerned with matters of translation and meaning, she does not engage such reading as a pedagogical issue.

As part of a politics of representation, photographic images necessitate the ability to read critically and to utilize particular analytical skills that enable viewers to study the relations among images, discourses, everyday life, and broader structures of power. As both the subject and object of public pedagogy, photographs deploy power and are deployed by power, and register the conditions under which people learn how to read texts and the world. Photographs demand an ability to read within and against their representations and to raise fundamental questions about how they work to secure particular meanings, desires, and investments. As a form of public pedagogy, photographic images have the potential—though it is by no means guaranteed—to call forth from readers modes of witnessing that connect meaning with compassion, a concern for others, and a broader understanding of the historical and contemporary contexts and relations that frame meaning in particular ways. Critical reading demands pedagogical practices that challenge common sense, resist easy assumptions, bracket how images are framed, engage meaning as a struggle over power and politics, and, as such, refuse to view reading (especially reading images) exclusively as an aesthetic exercise, but also as a political and moral one.

EDUCATION AFTER ABU GHRAIB

What is often ignored in the debates about Abu Ghraib—both in terms of its causes and what can be done about it—are questions that foreground the relevance of critical education to the debate. Such questions would clearly focus, at the very least, on what pedagogical conditions must be in place to enable people to view the images of abuse at Abu Ghraib prison not as part of a voyeuristic, even pornographic, reception, but through a variety of discourses that enable them to ask critical and probing questions that get at the heart of how people learn to participate in sadistic acts of abuse and torture, internalize racist assumptions that make it easier to dehumanize people different from themselves, accept commands that violate basic human rights, become indifferent to the suffering and hardships of others, and view dissent as basically unpatriotic. What pedagogical practices might enable the public to foreground the codes and structures that give photographs their meaning while also connecting the productive operations of photography with broader discourses? For example, how might the images from Abu Ghraib prison be understood as part of a broader debate about dominant information networks that condone torture and play a powerful role in organizing society around shared fears rather than shared responsibilities? Photographs demand more than a response to the specificity of an image; they also raise fundamentally crucial questions about the sites of pedagogy and technologies that produce, distribute, and frame them in particular ways, and what these operations mean in terms of how they resonate with historical and established relations of power and with the identities and modes of agency that enable such relations to be reproduced rather than resisted and challenged. Engaging the photographs from Abu Ghraib and the events that produced them would point to the pedagogical practice of foregrounding "the cultures of circulation and transfiguration within which those texts, events, and practices become palpable and are recognized as such."[60] For instance, how do we understand the Abu Ghraib images and the pedagogical conditions that produced them without engaging the discourses of privatization, particularly the contracting of military labour, the intersection of militarism and the crisis of masculinity, and the war on terrorism and the racism that makes it so despicable? How might one explain the ongoing evaporation of political dissent and opposing viewpoints in the United States that proceeded the events at Abu Ghraib without engaging the pedagogical campaign of fear-mongering adorned with the appropriate patriotic rhetoric waged by the Bush administration? How might we pedagogically "remember" a historical context for linking Abu Ghraib to a long legacy of abuse? More specifically, as the Palestinian-Jordanian journalist, Rami Kouri, argues: What might Abu Ghraib tell us about "autocratic power structures that have controlled, humiliated, and ultimately dehumanized Arab citizens for most of the past century of modern statehood—whether those powers were European colonial administrations, indigenous Arab elites, occupying Israeli forces, or the current Anglo-American managers of Iraq"?[61]

I have spent some time on suggesting that there is a link between how we translate images and pedagogy because I am concerned about what the events of Abu Ghraib prison might suggest about education as both the subject and object of a democratic society, and how we might engage it differently. What kind of education connects pedagogy and its diverse sites to the formation of a critical citizenry capable of challenging the on-going quasi-militarization of everyday life, the growing assault on secular democracy, the collapse of politics into a permanent war against terrorism, and the growing culture of fear increasingly used by political extremists to sanction the unaccountable exercise of presidential power? What kinds of educational practices can provide the conditions for a culture of question-ing and engaged civic action? What might it mean to rethink the educa-tional foundation of politics so as to reclaim not only the crucial traditions of dialogue and dissent, but also critical modes of agency and those public spaces that enable collectively engaged struggle? How might education be understood as a task of translation but also as a foundation for enabling civic engagement? What new forms of education might be called forth to resist the conditions and complicities that have allowed most people to sub-mit "so willingly to a new political order organized around fear"?[62] What does it mean to imagine a future beyond "permanent war," beyond a cul-ture of fear and the triumphalism that promotes the sordid demands of empire? How might education be used to question the official arguments legitimating the war on terrorism or to rouse citizens to challenge the so-cial, political, and cultural conditions that led to the horrible events of Abu Ghraib? Just as crucially, we must ponder the limits of education. Is there a point where extreme conditions short-circuit our moral instincts and abil-ity to think and act rationally? If this is the case, what responsibility do we have to challenge the reckless violence-as-first-resort ethos of the Bush administration?

Such questions extend beyond the events of Abu Ghraib. At the same time, Abu Ghraib provides an opportunity to connect the sadistic treatment of Iraqi prisoners to the tasks of redefining pedagogy as an ethical practice and of reconsidering the sites in which pedagogy takes place, and to the consequences of pedagogy for rethinking the meaning of politics in the twenty-first century. In order to confront the pedagogical and political challenges arising from the reality of Abu Ghraib, I want to revisit a classic essay by Theodor Adorno in which he tries to grapple with the relationship between education and morality in light of the horrors of Auschwitz. While I am certainly not equating the genocidal acts that took place at Auschwitz with the abuses at Abu Ghraib, a completely untenable analogy, I do believe that Adorno's essay offers some important theoretical insights about how to think about the larger meaning and purpose of education as a form of public pedagogy in light of the Abu Ghraib prison scandal. Adorno's essay raises fundamental questions about how acts of inhumanity are inextricably connected to the pedagogical practices that shape the conditions that bring them into being. Adorno insists that crimes against humanity cannot be reduced to the behaviour of a few individuals, but often speak in profound ways to the role of the state in propagating such abuses, to the mechanisms employed in the realm of culture that silence the public in the face of horrible acts, and to the pedagogical challenge that would name such acts as a moral crime against humankind and translate that moral authority into effective pedagogical practices throughout society so that such events never happen again. Of course, the significance of Adorno's comments extends far beyond matters of responsibility for what happened at Abu Ghraib prison. Adorno's plea for education as a moral and political force against human injustice is just as relevant today as it was following the revelations about Auschwitz after World War II. As Roger W. Smith points out, genocidal acts claimed the lives of over sixty million people in the twentieth century, sixteen million of them since 1945.[63] The political and economic forces fuelling such crimes against humanity—whether they are unlawful wars, systemic torture, practised indifference to chronic starvation and disease, or genocidal acts—are always mediated by educational forces, just as the resistance to such acts cannot take place without a degree of knowledge and self-reflection about how to name these acts and how to transform moral outrage into concrete attempts to prevent such human violations from taking place in the first place.

Education after Abu Ghraib

In 1967, Theodor Adorno published an essay titled "Education After Auschwitz." In it, he asserted that the demands and questions raised by Auschwitz had so barely penetrated the consciousness of people's minds that the conditions that made it possible continued, as he put it, "largely unchanged."[64] Mindful that the societal pressures that produced the Holocaust had far from receded in post-war Germany and that under such circumstances this act of barbarism could easily be repeated in the future,

Adorno argued that "the mechanisms that render people capable of such deeds"[65] must be made visible. For Adorno, the need to come to grips with the challenges arising from the reality of Auschwitz was both a political question and a crucial educational consideration. He recognized that education had to be an important part of any politics that took seriously its task to never allow another Auschwitz. As he put it:

> All political instruction finally should be centered upon the idea that Auschwitz should never happen again. This would be possible only when it devotes itself openly, without fear of offending any authorities, to this most important of problems. To do this, education must transform itself into sociology, that is, it must teach about the societal play of forces that operates beneath the surface of political forms.[66]

Implicit in Adorno's argument is the recognition that education as a critical practice could provide the means for disconnecting commonsense learning from the narrowly ideological impact of mass media, the regressive tendencies associated with hyper-masculinity, the rituals of everyday violence, the inability to identify with others, and the pervasive ideologies of state repression and its illusions of empire. Adorno's response to retrograde ideologies and practices was to emphasize the role of autonomous individuals and the force of self-determination, which he saw as the outcome of a moral and political project that rescued education from the narrow language of skills, unproblematized authority, and the seduction of commonsense assumptions. Self-reflection, the ability to call things into question, and the willingness to resist the material and symbolic forces of domination were central to an education that refused to repeat the horrors of the past and engaged the possibilities of the future. Adorno urged educators to teach students how to be critical, to learn how to resist those ideologies, needs, social relations, and discourses that lead back to a politics where authority is simply obeyed and the totally administered society reproduces itself through a mixture of state force and often orchestrated consensus. Freedom in this instance meant being able to think critically and act courageously, even when confronted with the limits of one's knowledge. Without such thinking, critical debate and dialogue degenerate into slogans; and politics, disassociated from the search for justice, becomes a power grab. Within the realm of education, Adorno glimpsed the possibility of knowledge for self and social formation as well as the importance of pedagogical practices capable of "influencing the the next generation of Germans so that they would not repeat what their parents or grandparents had done."[67]

Adorno realized that education played a crucial role in promoting consensus and creating the psychological, intellectual, and social conditions that made the Holocaust possible, yet he refused to dismiss education as an institution and set of social practices exclusively associated with domination. He argued that those theorists who viewed education simply as a tool for social reproduction had succumbed to the premier supposition of any oppressive hegemonic ideology: nothing can change. To dismiss the political and critical force of pedagogy, according to Adorno, was to fall prey to a disastrous determinism and a complicitous cynicism. He argues:

For this disastrous state of conscious and unconscious thought

139

includes the erroneous idea that one's own particular way of being—that one is just so and not otherwise—is nature, an unal-
terable given, and not a historical evolution. I mentioned the
concept of reified consciousness. Above all this is a consciousness blinded to all historical past, all insight into one's own con-
ditionedness, and posits as absolute what exists contingently.
If this coercive mechanism were once ruptured, then, I think,
something would indeed be gained.[68]

Realizing that education in Germany before and after Auschwitz
was separated by an unbridgeable chasm, Adorno wanted to invoke the
promise of education through the moral and political imperative of never
allowing the genocide witnessed at Auschwitz to happen again. For such a
goal to become meaningful and realizable, Adorno contended that education had to be addressed as both a promise and project in order to reveal
the conditions that laid the psychological and ideological groundwork for
Auschwitz, and to defeat the "potential for its recurrence."[69]

Investigating the powerful role that education, along with the conscious and unconscious elements of fascism, played to promote consensus
among the public, he understood education as more than social engineering
and argued that it also had to be imagined as a democratic public sphere. In
this context, education would take on a liberating and empowering function, refusing to substitute critical learning for mind-deadening training.[70]
At its best, such an education would create the pedagogical conditions in
which individuals would function as autonomous subjects capable of refusing to participate in unspeakable injustices while actively working to elimi-

nate the conditions that make such injustices possible. Human autonomy through self-reflection and social critique became, for Adorno, the basis for developing forms of critical agency as a means of resisting and overcoming both fascist ideology and identification with what he calls the fascist collective. According to Adorno, fascism as a form of barbarism defies all educational attempts at self-formation, engaged critique, self-determination, and transformative engagement. He writes: "The only true force against the principle of Auschwitz would be human autonomy ... that is, the force of reflection and of self-determination, the will to refuse participation."[71] While there is a deep-seated tension between Adorno's belief in the increasing power of the totally administered society, and his call for modes of education that produce critical, engaging, and free minds, he still believed that without critical education it was impossible to think about politics and agency, especially in light of the new technologies and material processes of social integration. Similarly, Adorno did not believe that education as an act of self-reflection alone could defeat the institutional forces and relations of power that existed beyond institutionalized education and other powerful sites of pedagogy in the larger culture, though he rightly acknowledged that changing such a powerful complex of economic and social forces begins with the educational task of recognizing that such changes are necessary and could actually be carried out through individual and collective forms of resistance. What Adorno brilliantly understood—though in a somewhat limited way, given his tendency, in the end, toward pessimism—was the necessity to link politics to matters of individual and social agency.[72] Engaging this relationship, in part, meant theorizing what it meant to make the political more pedagogical; that is, trying to understand how the very processes of learning constitute the political mechanisms through which identities—individual and collective—are shaped, desired, mobilized, experienced, and take on form and meaning within those formations that provide the educational foundation for constituting the realm of the social.

While it would be presumptuous to suggest that Adorno's writings on education, autonomy, and Auschwitz can be directly applied to theorizing the events at Abu Ghraib prison, his work offers some important theoretical insights for addressing how education might help to rethink the project of politics that made Abu Ghraib possible, as well as how violence and torture become normalized as part of the war on terrorism and the global war on all others considered marginal to American culture and life.

Recognizing how crucial education was in shaping everyday life and the conditions that made critique both possible and necessary, Adorno insisted that the desire for freedom and liberation was a function of pedagogy and could not be assumed a priori. At the same time, he was acutely aware that education took place both in schools and in larger public spheres, especially in the realm of media. Democratic debate and the conditions for autonomy grounded in a critical notion of individual and social agency could take place only if the schools addressed their important role in a democracy. Hence, Adorno argued that the critical education of teachers was essential in preventing dominant power from eliminating reflective thought and engaged social action. Such an insight appears particularly important at a time when public education is being privatized, commercialized, and test-driven, or, if it serves underprivileged students of colour, turned into disciplinary apparatuses that resemble prisons.[73] Public schools are under attack precisely because they have the potential to become democratic public spheres instilling in students the skills, knowledge, and values necessary for them to be critical citizens, capable of making power accountable and knowledge an intense object of dialogue and engagement. Of course, the attack on public education is increasingly taking place along with an attack on higher education, particularly the humanities.[74] Everything from affirmative action to academic freedom is up for grabs as neo-conservatives, religious fundamentalists, free-market missionaries, and hard-core right-wing ideologues (such as David Horowitz) have organized to impose political quotas on higher education by making conservative ideology a basis for faculty hires,[75] have introduced "ideological diversity" legislation that would cut federal funding for colleges and universities harbouring faculty and students who criticize Israel,[76] and have attacked curricula and faculty for being too liberal. Shrouded in the language of diversity and academic freedom, a mode of censorship is emerging in the United States with which Adorno had first-hand experience in Germany. The fascist censor not only presupposes that a person's political ideology translates into a rigid pedagogical script, but also that some ideas are actually dangerous and might influence people to think more critically about their own views, and the positions of others. Critical thinking coded as leftist thought is now viewed as a pathology, a form of contamination that will infect the minds of students too weak to defend or engage their own views, and may corrupt the nation as well.[77] Conservatives and liberals alike now believe that balance is more important as an academic principle than rigourous scholarship, and, consequently, support the spurious notion that faculty should be hired on the basis of their ideological positions rather than the excellence of their scholarship. What seems to be lost here is the recognition that fascism and censorship, not academic freedom, are the consequence of politicizing faculty hires and policing faculty thought according to a right-wing political litmus test.[78] If Adorno is right about educating teachers to neither forget nor allow horrors such as Auschwitz to happen again, the struggle over public and higher education as a democratic public sphere must be defended against base right-wing attacks. What is at stake here is more than a defense of academic freedom; it is a much-needed collective resistance to an attack on the very possibility of critical thought, civic courage, and the university as a place that encourages students to think and act as engaged democratic citizens.

At the same time, how we educate teachers for all levels of schooling must be viewed as more than a technical or credentialized task. It must be seen as a pedagogical practice of both learning and unlearning. Drawing upon Freudian psychology, Adorno believed that educators had to be educated to think critically and to avoid becoming the mediators and perpetrators of social violence. This meant addressing their psychological deformations by making clear the ideological, social, and material mechanisms that encourage people to participate or fail to intervene in such deeds. Pedagogy, in this instance, in addition to being concerned with learning particular modes of knowledge, skills, and self-reflection, was also concerned with addressing those dominant sedimented needs and desires that allowed teachers to blindly identify with repressive collectives and unreflectingly mimic their values while venting acts of hate and aggression.[79] If unlearning as a pedagogical practice meant resisting those social deformations that shaped everyday needs and desires, critical learning meant making visible those social practices and mechanisms that represented the opposite of self-formation and autonomous thinking with the goal of resisting such forces and preventing them from exercising power and influence.

Adorno realized far more than did Freud that the range and scope, not to mention the impact, of education had far exceeded the boundaries of public and higher education. Adorno increasingly believed that the media as a force for learning constituted a mode of public pedagogy that had to be criticized for discouraging critical reflection and reclaimed as a crucial force in providing the "intellectual, cultural, and social climate in which a recurrence [such as Auschwitz] would no longer be possible, a climate, therefore in which the motives that led to the horror would become relatively conscious."[80] Adorno rightly understood and critically engaged the media as a mode of public pedagogy, arguing that they contributed greatly to particular forms of barbarization, and that educators and others must "consider the impact of modern mass media on a state of consciousness."[81] If we are to take Adorno seriously, the role of the media in inspiring fear and hatred of Muslims and Arabs, and suppressing dissent regarding the US invasion and occupation of Iraq, and the media's determining influence in legitimating a number of myths and lies by the Bush administration, must be addressed as part of the larger set of concerns leading to the horror of Abu Ghraib. The media have consistently refused, for example, to comment critically on the ways in which the United States, in its flaunting of the Geneva Conventions regarding torture, was breaking international law, favouring instead the discourse of national security provided by the Bush administration. The media have also put into place forms of jingoism, patriotic correctness, and narrow-minded chauvinism, and a celebration of militarization that rendered dissent as treason, while the tortures at Abu Ghraib remain outside the discourses of ethics, compassion, human rights, and social justice.

Adorno also insisted that the global evolution of the media, and new technologies that shrank distances as they eroded face-to-face contact (and hence enhanced the ability to disregard the consequences of one's actions), had created a climate in which rituals of violence had become so entrenched in the culture that "aggression, brutality, and sadism" had become a normalized part of everyday life. The result was a twisted and pathological relationship with the body that not only tends toward violence, but also promotes what Adorno called the "ideology of hardness." Hardness, in this instance, referred to a notion of masculinity in which:

> virility consists in the maximum degree of endurance [that] aligns itself all too easily with sadism.... [and inflicts] physical

pain—often unbearable pain—upon a person as the price that must be paid in order to consider oneself a member, one of the collective. ... Being hard, the vaunted quality education should inculcate, means absolute indifference toward pain as such. In this, the distinction between one's pain and that of another is not so stringently maintained. Whoever is hard with himself earns the right to be hard with others as well and avenges himself for those manifestations he was not allowed to show and had to repress.[82]

The rituals of popular culture, especially reality television programs like *Survivor, The Apprentice*, and *Fear Factor*, and the new vogue of extreme sports, either condense pain, humiliation, and abuse into digestible spectacles of violence,[83] or serve up an endless celebration of retrograde competitiveness, the compulsion to "go it alone," the ideology of hardness, and power over others as the central features of masculinity. Masculinity in this context treats lies, manipulation, and violence as a sport that lets men connect with each other at some primal level in which the pleasure of the body, pain, and competitive advantage are maximized while violence is close to acquiring a glamorous and fascist edge.

The celebration of both violence and hardness (witness the fanfare over Donald Trump's tag line "you're fired!") can also be seen in those ongoing representations and images that accompany the simultaneous erosion of security (health care, work, education) and the militarization of everyday life. The United States has more police, prisons, spies, weapons, and soldiers than at any time in its history—coupled with a growing "army" of the unemployed and incarcerated. Yet, its military is enormously popular, as its underlying values, social relations, and patriotic, hyper-masculine aesthetic spread out into other aspects of American culture. The ideology of hardness, toughness, and hyper-masculinity is constantly disseminated through a militarized culture that functions as a mode of public pedagogy, instilling the values and the aesthetic of militarization through a wide variety of pedagogical sites and cultural venues.

The ideology of hardness and hyper-masculinity in its present form also speaks to a discontinuity with the era in which the crimes of Auschwitz were committed. As Zygmunt Bauman has pointed out to me in a private correspondence, Auschwitz was a closely guarded secret of which even the Nazis were ashamed. Such a secret could not be defended in light of bourgeois morality (even as it made Auschwitz possible); but in the current morality of downsizing, punishment, violence, and kicking the excluded, the infliction of humiliation, pain, and abuse on those considered weak or less clever is not only celebrated, but also served up as a daily ritual of cultural life. Such practices, especially through the proliferation of "reality" television, have become so familiar that the challenge for any kind of critical education is to recognize that the conduct of those involved in the abuse at Abu Ghraib was neither shocking nor unique. Hence, the ideology of hardness is far more pervasive today and poses much more difficult challenges educationally and politically.[84]

From video games to clothing to magazines, popular culture increasingly produces representations of masculinity and violence that mimic fascism's militarization of the public sphere, where physical aggression is a crucial element of male bonding and violence is the ultimate language, referent, and currency through which to understand how, as Susan Sontag has suggested in another context, politics "dissolves…into pathology."[85] Such militarized pedagogies play a powerful role in producing identities and modes of agency completely at odds with those elements of autonomy, critical reflection, and social justice that Adorno privileged in his essay. Adorno's ideology of hardness, when coupled with neoliberal values that aggressively promote a Hobbesian world based on fear, the narrow pursuit of individual interests, and an embrace of commodified relations, profoundly influences individuals who seem increasingly indifferent towards the pain of others, pit their own ambitions against those of everyone else, and assimilate themselves to things, numb to those principles that hail us as moral witnesses and call for us to do something about human suffering. Adorno suggests that the inability to identify with others was one of the root causes of Auschwitz:

> The inability to identify with others was unquestionably the most important psychological condition for the fact that something like Auschwitz could have occurred in the midst of more or less civilised and innocent people. What is called fellow travelling was primarily business interest: one pursues one's own advantage before all else, and simply not to endanger oneself, does not talk too much. That is a general law of the status quo. The silence under the terror was only its consequence. The coldness of the societal monad, the isolated competitor, was the precondition, as indifference to the fate of others, for the fact that only

> very few people reacted. The torturers know this, and they put
> it to test ever anew.[86]

Adorno's prescient analysis of the role of education after Auschwitz is particularly important in examining those values, ideologies, and pedagogical forces at work in American culture that suggest that Abu Ghraib is not an aberration as much as an outgrowth of those dehumanizing and demonizing ideologies and social relations characteristic of an expanding market fundamentalism, militarism, and nationalism. While these are not the only forces that contributed to the violations that took place at Abu Ghraib, they do point to how particular manifestations of hyper-masculinity, violence, militarization, and jingoistic patriotism are elaborated through forms of public pedagogy that produce identities, social relations, and values conducive to both the ambitions of empire and the cruel and degrading treatment of those who are its victims. What ultimately drives the ideological vision behind these practices, what provides a stimulus for abuse and sanctioned brutality, is the presupposition that a particular society is above the law, either indebted only to God, as John Ashcroft has insisted, or rightfully scornful of those individuals and cultures undeserving of human rights because they have been labelled part of an evil empire or dismissed as terrorists.[87] The educational force of these ideological practices allows state power to be held unaccountable while legitimizing an "indifference to the concerns and the suffering of people in places remote from our Western metropolitan sites of self-interest."[88]

Adorno believed that the authoritarian tendencies in capitalism were creating individuals who made a cult out of efficiency, suffered from emotional callousness, had a tendency to treat other human beings as things, and reproduced the ultimate expressions of reification under capitalism. The grip that these pathogenic traits had on the German populace then and the American public today can, in part, be explained by the inability of people to recognize that such traits are conditioned rather than determined. In keeping with Adorno's reasoning, such traits, even when seen as an intolerable given, are often posited as an absolute, "something that blinds itself toward any process of having come into being, toward any insight into our own conditionality."[89] Adorno's insights regarding the educational force of late capitalism to construct individuals who were cold through and through, and incapable of empathizing with the plight of others, are theoretically useful in illuminating some of the conditions that contributed to the abuses that took place at Abu Ghraib. Adorno was particularly prescient in forecasting the connection between the subjective mechanisms that produce political indifference and racialized intolerance, the all-encompassing market fundamentalism of neoliberal ideology, and a virulent nationalism that feeds on the pieties of theocratic pretentiousness, and the relationship of all of these elements to an escalating authoritarianism. What is remarkable about his analysis is that it appears to apply equally well to the United States.

The signals are everywhere. Under the current reign of free-market fundamentalism, capital and wealth have largely been distributed upwards while civic virtue has been undermined by a celebration of the free market as the model for organizing all facets of everyday life. Financial investments, market identities, and commercial values take precedence over human needs, public responsibilities, and democratic relations. With its debased beliefs that profit-making is the essence of democracy and that citizenship should be defined by an energized plunge into consumerism, market fundamentalism eliminates government regulation of big business, celebrates a ruthless competitive individualism, and places the commanding institutions of society in the hands of powerful corporate interests, the privileged, and unrepentant religious bigots. Under such circumstances, individuals are viewed as privatized consumers rather than public citizens. As the Bush administration rolls American society back to the Victorian capitalism of the robber barons, social welfare is viewed as a drain on corporate profits that should be eliminated, while at the same time the development of the economy is left to the wisdom of the market. Market fundamentalism destroys politics by commercializing public spheres and rendering politics corrupt and cynical.[90]

The impoverishment of public life is increasingly matched by the impoverishment of thought itself, particularly as the media substitutes patriotic cheerleading for real journalism.[91] The cloak of patriotism is now cast over retrograde social policies and a coercive unilateralism in which military force has replaced democratic idealism; and war has become the organizing principle of society—a source of pride—rather than a source of alarm. In the face of massive corruption, the erosion of civil liberties, and a spreading culture of fear, the defining feature of politics seems to be its insignificance, as it is reduced to an ideology and practice that celebrate passivity and cynicism while promoting conformity and collective impotence.[92] For many, the collapse of democratic life and politics is paid for in the hard currency of isolation, poverty, inadequate health care, impoverished schools, and the loss of decent employment.[93] Within this regime of symbolic and material capital, the other—figured as a social drain on the accumulation of wealth—is feared, exploited, reified, or considered disposable, and rarely is the relationship between the self and the other mediated by compassion and empathy.[94]

But market fundamentalism does more than destroy the subjective conditions for autonomous political agency and an ethical concern for fellow citizens; it also shreds the social order as it threatens destruction abroad. Cornel West points out:

> Free market fundamentalism—the basic dogma across the globe—is producing obscene levels of wealth and inequality around the world. Market as idol. Corporation as fetish. Acting as if workers are just appendages or some kind of market calculation. Outsourcing here, outsourcing there. Ascribing magical powers to the market and thinking it can solve all problems. When free market fundamentalism is tied to escalating authoritarianism, it results in increasing surveillance of citizens and monitoring of classes at universities and colleges. When it is tied to aggressive militarism, we get not just invasion of those countries perceived to be threats, but a military presence in 132 countries, a ship in every ocean.[95]

We also get the privatized armies of mercenaries that take over traditional military functions, from cooking meals to interrogating prisoners. In Iraq, it has been estimated that "for every ten troops on the ground ... there is one contract employee. That translates into 10,000 to 15,000 contract workers, making them the second-largest contingent (between American and Britain) of the 'coalition of the willing.'"[96] Firms such as Erinys and CACI International provide rental Rambos, some of whom have notorious backgrounds as mercenaries for hire. One widely reported incident involved two civilian contractors blown up by a suicide bomber in Baghdad in the winter of 2003. Both were South Africans who belonged to a terrorist organization infamous for killing blacks, terrorizing anti-apartheid activists, and paying a bounty on the bodies of black activists.[97] In Iraq, Steve Stefanowicz, a civilian interrogator employed by CACI International, was cited in the Taguba report as having "'allowed and/or instructed' MPs to abuse and humiliate Iraqi prisoners and as giving orders that he knew 'equated to physical abuse.'"[98] While the Justice Department has opened up a criminal investigation on an unnamed civilian contractor in Iraq, CACI has refused to take action against Stefanowicz, making clear the charge that private contractors are not monitored as closely as military personnel and are not subject to the same Congressional and public oversights and scrutiny. The lack of democratic accountability results in more than bungled services and price gouging by Halliburton, Bechtel, Northrop Grumman, and other corporations that have become familiar news items; it also results in human rights abuses organized under the logic of "rationalizing" and market efficiency. Journalist Tim Shorrock claims that "The military's abuse of Iraqi prisoners is bad enough, but the privatization of such practices is simply intolerable."[99]

The pedagogical implications of Adorno's analysis of the relationship between authoritarianism and capitalism suggest that any viable educational project would have to recognize how market fundamentalism has not only damaged democratic institutions, but has also compromised the ability of people to identify with democratic social formations and invest in crucial public goods, let alone reinvigorate the concept of compassion as an antidote to the commodity-driven view of human relationships. Adorno understood that critical knowledge alone could not adequately address the deformations of mind and character put into place by the subjective mechanisms of capitalism. Instead, he argued that critical knowledge had to be reproduced and democratic social experiences put into place through shared values and practices that create inclusive and compassionate communities which make democratic politics possible and safeguard the autonomous subject through the creation of needs that are non-oppressive. Within the boundaries of critical education, students have to learn the skills and knowledge to narrate their own stories, resist the fragmentation and seductions of market ideologies, and create shared pedagogical sites that extend the range of democratic politics. Ideas gain relevance in terms of whether and how they enable students to participate in the worldly sphere of self-criticism and the publicness of everyday life. Theory and knowledge, in other words, become a force for autonomy and self-determination within the space of public engagement, and their significance is based less on a self-proclaimed activism than on their ability to make critical and thoughtful connections "beyond theory, within the space of politics itself."[100] Adorno's educational project for autonomy recognizes the necessity of a worldly space in which freedom is allowed to make its appearance, a space that is both the condition and the object of struggle for any viable form of critical pedagogy. Such a project also understands the necessity of compassion to remind people of the full humanity and suffering of others, as well as of "the importance of compassion in shaping the civic imagination."[101] If Adorno is correct, and I think he is, his call to refashion education in order to prevent inhuman acts has to take as one of its founding tasks today the necessity to understand how free market ideology, privatization, outsourcing, and the relentless drive for commodified public space radically diminish those political and pedagogical sites crucial for sustaining democratic identities, values, and practices.

Adorno's critique of nationalism appears as useful today as it did when it appeared in the late 1960s. He believed that those forces pushing an aggressive nationalism harboured a distinct rage against divergent groups who stood at odds with such imperial ambitions. Intolerance and militarism, according to Adorno, fuelled a nationalism that became "pernicious because in the age of international communication and supranational blocks it cannot completely believe in itself anymore and has to exaggerate boundlessly in order to convince itself and others that it is still substantial ... [Moreover] movements of national renewal in an age when nationalism is outdated, seem to be especially susceptible to sadistic practices."[102] Surely, such a diagnosis would fit the imperial ambitions of Richard Cheney, Richard Perle, Donald Rumsfeld, Paul Wolfowitz, and other neo-conservatives whose dreams of empire are entirely at odds with both a desire to preserve human dignity or a respect for international law. Convinced that the US should not only maintain political and military dominance in the post-cold-war world, but also prevent any nation or alliance from challenging its superiority, nationalists across the ideological spectrum advocate a discourse of exceptionalism that calls for a dangerous unity at home and reckless imperial ambitions abroad. Belief in empire has come to mean that the US would now shape rather than react to world events and act decisively in using "its overwhelming military and economic might to create conditions conducive to American values and interests."[103] American unilateralism buttressed by the dangerous doctrine of preemption has replaced multilateral diplomacy; religious fundamentalism has found its counterpart in the ideological messianism of neo-conservative designs on the rest of the globe; and a knee-jerk moralism that divides the world into good and evil has replaced the possibility of dialogue and debate. Within such a climate, blind authority demands as it rewards authoritarian behaviour so as to make power and domination appear beyond the pale of criticism or change, providing the political and educational conditions for eliminating self-reflection and compassion even in the face of the most sadistic practices and imperial ambitions.

American support for the invasions of Iraq and the apartheid wall in Israel as well as targeted assassinations and torture are now defended in the name of righteous causes even by liberals such as Niall Ferguson, Paul Berman, and Michael Ignatieff, who, like their neo-conservative counterparts, revel in the illusion that American power can be used as a force for progress, in spite of the official terror and reckless suffering it imposes on much of the world.[104] National justification for the most messianic militaristic policies, as indicated by the war in Iraq, is wrapped up in the discourse of democracy and divine mission, an updated version of American exceptionalism, in spite of the toll the war takes on Iraqi lives—mostly children—and young US soldiers. Then, there is the wasted $141 billion being spent on the war that could be used to support life-giving social programs at home. Even moderately liberal democrats now appeal to an uncritical chauvinism with a fervour equally matched by its ability to cheapen the most basic tenets of democracy and deaden in some of its citizens the obligation to be responsible to the suffering and hardships of those who exist outside its national borders. Barack Obama, a rising star in the Democratic Party and a keynote speaker at the 2004 Democratic convention, insisted we are "One America," a moniker that does more to hide contradictions and injustices than to invoke their continuing presence and the necessity to overcome them. Equally important, "One America," when appealed to outside a critical examination of the damaging chauvinism that informs such a call, ends up reproducing a more liberal, though equally privileged, notion of America's role in the world, a role that seems to have little understanding of what the limits might be or of the legacy of human suffering it has produced historically and continues to produce.

EDUCATION AFTER ABU GHRAIB

The aggressive nationalism that Adorno viewed as fundamental to the conditions that produced Auschwitz has not been laid to rest. Echoes of such jingoistic rhetoric can be heard from neoconservatives who want to wage a holy war against the non-Western hordes that threaten all things Christian, European, and civilized. This virulent nationalism can be heard in the semantic contortions justifying hard and soft versions of empire, often produced by conservative think-tanks and Ivy League intellectuals acting as modern-day missionaries for their corporate sponsors. It can be heard in the fundamentalist rhetoric of religious bigots such as Jerry Falwell and Pat Robertson, who are fanatically pro-Israel and are waging an incessant propaganda war for claiming Palestinian land in the name of Christian ideals. The discourse of empire finds a more tangible expression in the presence of 725 US military bases in 138 foreign countries that circle the globe.[105]

The discourse of empire must be deconstructed and replaced in our schools and other sites of pedagogy with new global models of democracy, models grounded in an ethics and morality in which the relationship between the self and others extends beyond the chauvinism of national boundaries and embraces a new and critical understanding of the interdependencies of the world and their implications for citizenship in global democracy. Memory must serve as a bulwark against the discourse of empire, which is often built on the erasure of historical struggles and conflicts. Memory in this instance is more than counter-knowledge; it is a form of resistance, a resource through which to wage pedagogical and political struggles to recover those narratives, traditions, and values that remind students and others of the graphic nature of suffering that unfolded in the aftermath of America's claims for a permanent war on terrorism. Appeals to American exceptionalism and the obligations of empire building sound hollow in the face of the monstrosities they produce, even as such appeals also legitimize a process of othering, excluding many from a narrow definition of which constitutes human dignity, human rights, and international law.

At the heart of Adorno's concern with education was the call to create pedagogical practices in which we supplement knowledge with self-criticism. Self- and social criticism was, for Adorno, a crucial element of autonomy, but criticism was not enough. Agency as a political force mattered in that it was not only capable of saying no to abusive power, but also because it could imagine itself as a mechanism for changing the world. As a condition of politics and collective struggle, agency requires being able to engage democratic values, principles, and practices as a force for resistance and hope in order to challenge unquestioned modes of authority while also enabling individuals to connect such principles and values to "the world in which they live as citizens."[106] Adorno's plea for education rests on the assumption that human beings make both knowledge and history, rather than both simply washing over them. For Adorno, critical reflection was the essence of all genuine education as well as politics. Ongoing reflection provided the basis for individuals to become autonomous by revealing the human origins of institutions and thereby the recognition that society could be open to critique and change. Politics is thus theorized as a practical effort to link freedom to agency in the service of extending the promise of democratic institutions, values, and social relations. The capacity for self-knowledge, self-critique, and autonomy becomes more powerful when it is nourished within pedagogical spaces and sites that refuse to be parochial, that embrace difference over bigotry, global democracy over chauvinism, peace over militarism, and secularism over religious fundamentalism. The urgency of such a call can be heard in William Greider's plea for critical education to bring the presidency of George W. Bush to an end:

> The only way out of this fog of pretension is painful self-examination by Americans—cutting our fears down to more plausible terms and facing the complicated realities of our role in the world. The spirited opposition that arose to Bush's war in Iraq is a good starting place, because citizens raised real questions that were brushed aside. I don't think that most Americans are interested in imperial rule, but they were grossly misled by patriotic rhetoric. Now is the time for sober, serious teach-ins that lay out the real history of US power in the world, and that also explain the positive and progressive future that is possible. Once citizens have constructed a clear-eyed, dissenting version of our situation, perhaps politicians can also be liberated from exaggerated fear. The self-imposed destruction that has flowed from Bush's logic cannot be stopped until a new cast of leaders steps forward to guide the country.[107]

Teach-ins, reading groups, public debates, and film screenings should take place in a variety of sites and spaces for dialogue and learning, and they should focus not simply on the imperial ambitions of the US, but also on the dehumanizing practices informed by a political culture in which human life that does not align itself with official power and corporate ideology is deemed disposable. The connection between Auschwitz and Abu Ghraib can also be traced in the educational force of popular culture in which pedagogy is disassociated from justice, citizenship is restricted to the obligations of consumerism, and compassion is dissolved in the mechanics of social Darwinism. As I emphasized previously, Abu Ghraib cannot be equated with the genocidal intent of Auschwitz, but the conditions that allowed Americans to commit such abuses on Iraqi detainees harbour the possibilities for atrocious acts of inhumanity, only this time they are dressed up in the rhetoric of advancing the democratic principles of freedom and justice. Adorno believed that education as a democratic force could play a central role in altering the rising tide of authoritarianism on a national and global level. His call to rethink the value and importance of education as a central element of politics offers an opportunity, especially for educators and other cultural workers, to learn from the horrors of Abu Ghraib, and to rethink the value of critical education and public pedagogy as an all-important part of politics, the future of public institutions, and global democracy itself. In addition, Adorno brilliantly understood that it was not enough to turn the tools of social critique simply upon the government or other apparatuses of domination. Critique also had to come to grips with the affective investments that tied individuals, including critics, to ideologies and practices of domination. Analyses of the deep structures of domination might help to provide a more powerful critique and healthy suspicion of various appeals to community, the public, and the social. Clearly, while it is imperative to reclaim the discourse of community, the commons, and public good as part of a broader discourse of democracy, such terms need to be embraced critically in light of the ways in which they have often served the instruments of dominant power.

Adorno was insistent that education was crucial as a point of departure for imagining autonomy, recognizing the interdependency of human life, and stopping cycles of violence. Education can help us to imagine a world in which violence can be minimized as well as to reject the disparagement, exclusion, and abuse of those deemed others in a social order in which one's worth is often measured through the privileged categories of gender, class, race, citizenship, and language. Education can also seek to identify and destroy the conditions that provide an outlet for murderous rage, hatred, fear, and violence. This requires a pedagogical commitment, in Judith Butler's eloquent words,

> to return us to the human where we do not expect to find it, in its frailty and at the limits of its capacity to make sense. We would have to interrogate the emergence and vanishing of the human at the limits of what we can know, what we can hear, what we can see, what we can sense. This might prompt us, affectively to reinvigorate the intellectual projects of critique of questioning, of coming to understand the difficulties and demands of cultural translation and dissent, and to create a sense of the public in which oppositional voices are not feared, degraded or dismissed, but valued for the instigation to a sensate democracy they oc-

casionally perform.[108]

But under certain circumstances, the limits of education have to be understood. What is difficult to grasp is that simply because one learns to be non-violent as part of a respect for humanity, a visceral repulsion for the suffering of others, or an ethical conception of mutual obligation, outbursts of violence cannot be entirely contained within such a rationality or mode of understanding. Under certain enormously stressful conditions, violence merges with circumstances of extreme social and bodily vulnerability and may appear to be one of the few options available for dealing with those already dismissed as inhuman or disposable.[109] Even more horrible is the possibility that inhuman acts of abuse under nerve-wracking conditions represent one of the few outlets for pleasure. Is it conceivable that under certain conditions of violence and stress, only the unthinkable is imaginable, that the only avenue for the release of pleasure can be attained by extending the logic of violence to those deemed as the other, those undeserving of narration, agency, and power? Under certain modes of domination with all its stress-inducing consequences, those who exercise a wanton and dehumanizing power often feel that everything is permissible because all the rules appear to have broken down. The stress soldiers sometime experience under such circumstances is often satisfied through the raw feel and exercise of power. Abu Ghraib remains, tragically, a terrible site of violence, a site in which an ethics of non-violence seems almost incomprehensible, given the tension, anxiety, and daily violence that framed what happened in the prison and in daily life in Iraq. Under these conditions, neither education nor an ethics of peace may be enough to prevent "fear and anxiety from turning into murderous action."[110] Under extreme conditions in which abuse, loss, hardship, and dehumanization shape the consciousness and daily routines of one's existence, whether it be for US soldiers working in Abu Ghraib or Israeli soldiers occupying Hebron, violence can undercut the appeal to ethics, critical reflection, and all educated sensibilities.[111] This is not to suggest education does not matter much in light of such conditions as much as to suggest, following Adorno's insight, that education must address what it means to prevent the conditions in which violence takes root and develops a life of its own.

As a political and moral practice, education must be engaged not only as one of the primary conditions for constructing political and moral agents, but also as a public pedagogy—produced in a range of sites and public spheres—that constitutes cultural practice as a defining feature of any viable notion of politics. Education after Abu Ghraib must imagine a future in which learning is inextricably connected to social change, the obligations of civic justice, and a notion of democracy in which peace, equality, compassion, and freedom are not limited to the nation-state but are extended to the international community. Education after Abu Ghraib must take seriously what it might mean to strive for the autonomy and dignity of a global citizenry and peace as its fundamental precondition.

AGAINST THE NEW AUTHORITARIANISM

1   I can no longer write without the presence and insights that Susan Giroux brings to my life and work. With great love and admiration, I thank her for the generous support and intellectual insights she provided while I was researching and writing this article.

2   Ronald Steel, "Fight Fire with Fire," *The New York Times Book Review* (July 25, 2004): 12-13.

3   For an interesting comment on how the Bush media team attempted to enhance his presidential persona through the iconography of conservative, hyped-up, macho-phallic masculinity, see Richard Goldstein, "Bush's Basket," *The Village Voice* (May 21-27, 2003). Available on-line: http://www.villagevoice.com/issues/0321/goldstein.php.

4   Susan Sontag, "Regarding the Torture of Others: Notes on what has been done—and why—to prisoners, by Americans," *The New York Times Sunday Magazine* (May 23, 2004): 26-27.

5   Sidney Blumenthal, "This Is the New Gulag," *The Guardian*, May 6, 2004. Available on-line: www.guardian.co.uk/print/0,38584917539-103677,00.html.

6   While I can't name all the relevant sources theorizing the ethical nature of torture or its use by the American military, some important recent contributions include: Seymour M. Hersh, "Torture at Abu Ghraib," *The New Yorker* (May 10, 2004): 42-47; Mark Danner, "Torture and Truth," *The New York Review of Books* (May 27, 2004): 46-50; Mark Danner, "The Logic of Torture," *The New York Review of Books* (June 24, 2004): 70-74; Anthony Lewis, "The US Case for Torture," *The New York Review of Books* (July 15, 2004): 4-8; Steven Strasser, ed. *The Abu Ghraib Investigations* (New York: Public Affairs, 2005); Karyn Greenburg and Joshua Drater, eds., *The Torture Papers: The Road to Abu Ghraib* (New York: Cambridge University Press, 2005).

7   Emily Bazelon, writing for *Mother Jones*, claims that "in December 2002 ... two detainees died in custody at the base. One was Mullah Habibullah, a 30-year-old man from the southern province of Oruzgan; the other was a 22-year-old taxi driver named Dilawar (many Afghans use only one name), who was married and had a 2-year-old daughter. The men had been hung by their arms from the ceiling and beaten so severely that, according to a report by Army investigators later leaked to the *Baltimore Sun,* their legs would have needed to be amputated had they lived. The Army's Criminal Investigation command launched an inquiry, but few people outside Afghanistan took notice." See Emily Bazelon, "From Bagram to Abu Ghraib," *Mother Jones* (March/April 2005): 56. Also see Edward T. Pound and Kit R. Roane, "Hell on Earth," *U.S.*

166

News and World Report (July 19, 2004). Available on-line: www.usnews.com/usnews/issue/040719/usnews/19prison.htm. Also see Editorial, "The Horror of Abu Ghraib," *The Nation*, May 24, 2004, 3. Degrading prisoners at Abu Ghraib had become so pervasive that forced nudity was seen as a commonplace phenomenon by both military personnel and detainees. See Kate Zernike and David Rohde, "Forced Nudity of Iraqi Prisoners Is Seen as a Pervasive Pattern, Not Isolated Incidents," *The New York Times*, June 8, 2004, A11.

8   Cited in Seymour Hersh, "Chain of Command," *The New Yorker* (May 17, 2004): 40.

9   Pound and Roane, "Hell on Earth."

10 Section of Taguba's report cited in Hersh, "Torture at Abu Ghraib."

11 Bush cited in Lisa Hajjar, "Torture and the Politics of Denial," *In These Times* (June 21, 2004): 12.

12 Katha Pollitt, "Show and Tell in Abu Ghraib," *The Nation* (May 24, 2004): 9.

13 Patricia J. Williams, "In Kind," *The Nation* (May 31, 2004): 10.

14 George Bush, "President Outlines Steps to Help Iraq Achieve Democracy and Freedom," Office of the White House Press Secretary (May 24, 2004). Available on-line: www.whitehouse.gov/news/releases/2004/05/20040524-10.html.

15 General Myers's remarks are cited in Dave Moniz and Tom Squitieri, "Lawyers Raised Questions and Concerns on Interrogations," *USA Today* (June 10, 2004): 13A.

16 Anthony Lewis, "Making Torture Legal," *The New York Review of Books* (July 15, 2004), 8.

17 The memo can be found on-line at: www.cooperativeresearch.org/entity.jsp?entity=draft_memo_to_the_president_from_alberto_gonzales,_january_25,_2004.

18 Lewis, "Making Torture Legal," 6.

19 Neil A. Lewis, "Bush Didn't Order Any Breach of Torture Laws, Ashcroft Says," *The New York Times,* June 9, 2004. Available on-line: www.nytimes.com/2004/06/09/politics.

20 Jess Bravin, "Pentagon Report Set Framework for Use of Torture," *Wall Street Journal*, June 7, 2004. Available on-line: www.commondreams.org/cgi-bin/print.cgi?file=/headlines04/0607-01.htm.

21 See Chapter One of the manual, "Interrogation and the Interrogator." Available on-

line: http://www.globalsecurity.org/intell/library/policy/army/fm/fm34-52/chapter1. htm.

22 Lewis, "Making Torture Legal," 4, 6.

23 Associated Press, "DOD Denies Report's Claims," *Military.Com* (May 16, 2004). Available on-line: http://www.military.com/NewsContent/0,13319,FL_rumsfeld_ 051604,00.html.

24 Cited in David Folkenflik, "Dodging Using Words Like 'Torture,'" *BaltimoreSun.Com* (May 26, 2004). Available on-line: http://www.baltimoresun.com/entertainment/tv/ bal-to.media26may26,0,7304614.column?coll=bal-artslife-tv.

25 Cited in Hersh, "Chain of Command."

26 Ibid.

27 Josh White and Scott Higham, "Use of Dogs to Scare Prisoners Was Authorized," *Washington Post*, June 11, 2004, A01.

28 Kate Zernke and David Rohde, "Forced Nudity of Iraqi Prisoners Is Seen as a Pervasive Pattern, Not Isolated Incidents," *New York Times*, June 8, 2004, A11.

29 Bob Drogin, "Most 'Arrested by Mistake'," *Los Angeles Times*, May 11, 2004. Available on-line: www.commondreams.org/cgi-bin/print.cgi?file=headlines04/0511-04.htm.

30 Ray McGovern, "Not Scared Yet? Try Connecting These Dots," *Common Dreams* (August 11, 2004). Available on-line: http://www.commondreams.org/views04/0809-11.htm.

31 Ibid.

32 Josh White and Thomas E. Ricks, "Iraqi Teens Abused at Abu Ghraib, Report Finds," *The Washington Post*, August 24, 2004, A01.

33 Maureen Dowd, "Torture Chicks Gone Wild," *The New York Times*, January 30, 2005, 17.

34 Jeannie Shawl, "Prostitutes Used in Gitmo Torture, Lawyer for Australian Detainee Says," *Jurist: Legal News and Research* (January 26, 2005). Available on-line: http://jurist.law.pitt.edu/paperchase/2005/01/prostitutes-used-in-gitmo-torture.php.

35 For a statement by Huda Alazawi, a female Iraqi detainee, on her horrific treatment at Abu Ghraib, see Luke Harding, "After Abu Ghraib," *The Guardian*, September 20, 2004. Available on-line: http://www.guardian.co.uk/print/0,3858,5019756-103680,00.html.

36 Eric Schmitt, "Defense Leaders Faulted by Panel in Prison Abuse," *The New York*

Times, August 24, 2004, 1.

37 Editorial, "Legalizing Torture," *The Washington Post*, June 9, 2004, A20.

38 Douglas Jehl and Eric Schmitt, "US Military Says 26 Inmate Deaths May Be Homicide," *The New York Times* (March 16, 2005), A9.

39 Ibid., A1.

40 Josh White, "General Promoted But Cleared in Abuse Probe." *Washington Post* (May 6, 2005) A08.

41 Fay Bowers, "The Message of Abu Ghraib," Christian Science Monitor (May 7, 2005) on-line: www.alternet.org/story/21955.

42 Norman Solomon, "The Coming Backlash Against Outrage," *Common Dreams* (May 12, 2004). Available on-line: www.commondreams.org/cgi-bin/print. cgi?file=views04/0512-05.htm.

43 All these examples are cited in Frank Rich, "It Was Porn that Made Them Do It," *New York Times*, May 30, 2004, AR1.

44 The level of secrecy employed by the Bush administration is both dangerous and absurd. For example, some individuals were shocked to learn that if they wanted to attend a rally hosted by Vice-President Dick Cheney at Rio Rancho Mid-High School in New Mexico the weekend of July 30, 2004, they could not get tickets to the rally unless they signed an endorsement pledging allegiance to President George W. Bush. See Jeff Jones, *Albuquerque Journal*, July 30, 2004, 1.

45 I take up many of these issues in greater detail in Henry A. Giroux, *The Terror of Neoliberalism: The New Authoritarianism and the Attack on Democracy* (Denver, CO: Paradigm Press, 2004).

46 Rich, "Porn Made Them Do It," AR1, AR16.

47 Cited in Gary Younge, "Blame the White Trash," *Guardian*, May 17, 2004. Available on-line: www.commondreams.org/cgi-bin/pring.cgi?file=/views04/0517-03.htm.

48 Cited in ibid.

49 Rich, "Porn Made Them Do It," AR1.

50 Andrew Sullivan, "The Abu Ghraib Investigations," *New York Times Book Review* (January 13, 2005), 18.

51 Sontag, "Regarding the Torture of Others," 25.

52 Sontag, *Regarding the Pain of Others* (New York: Farrar, Straus and Giroux, 2003), 26.

53 For an excellent discussion of this issue, see John Louis Lucaites and James P. Mc-Daniel, "Telescopic Mourning/Warring in the Global Village: Decomposing (Japanese) Authority Figures," *Communication and Critical/Cultural Studies* 1, no.1 (March 2004): 1-28.

54 This issue is taken up brilliantly in Abigail Solomon-Godeau, *Photography at the Dock* (Minnesota: University of Minnesota Press, 1994).

55 Jeffrey R. DiLeo, Walter Jacobs, and Amy Lee, "The Sites of Pedagogy," *Symploke* 10, no.1-2: 9.

56 Hazel Carby, "A Strange and Bitter Crop: The Spectacle of Torture," *Open Democracy* (October 11, 2004). Available on-line: http://www.opendemocracy.net/content/articles/PDF/2149.pdf?redirect2=/debates/article-8-112-2149.jsp.

57 Lucaites and McDaniel, "Telescopic Mourning," 7.

58 Arthur C. Danto, "American Self-Consciousness in Politics and Art," *Artforum* (September 2004). Available on-line: http://www.artforum.com/inprint/id=7391.

59 Judith Butler, "Explanation and Exoneration, or What We Can Hear," *Theory & Event* 5,4 (2002): 19.

60 Dilip Parameshwar Gaonkar and Elizabeth A. Povinelli, "Technologies of Public Forms: Circulation, Transfiguration, Recognition," *Public Culture* 15, no.3 (2003): 386.

61 Rami Kouri, "Abu Ghraib in the Arab Mirror," *Open Democracy* (October 19, 2004). Available on-line: http://www.opendemocracy.net/debates/article-8-112-2166.jsp.

62 William Greider, "Under the Banner of the 'War' on Terror," *The Nation* (June 21, 2004), 14.

63 Roger W. Smith, "American Self-Interest and the Response to Genocide," *The Chronicle Review* (July 30, 2004). Available on-line: http://chronicle.com/cgi2-bin/printible.cgi?article=http://chronicle.com.

64 This was first presented as a radio lecture on April 18, 1966, under the title "Padagogik nack Auschwitz." The first published version appeared in 1967. The English translation appears as "Education after Auschwitz," Theodor Adorno, *Critical Models: Interventions and Catchwords* (New York: Columbia University Press, 1998): 191.

65 Ibid., 192.

66 Ibid., 203.

67 Peter Hohendahl, "Education After the Holocaust," in *Prismatic Thought: Theodor*

Adorno (Lincoln, Nebraska: University of Nebraska Press, 1995): 51.

68 Adorno, "Education after Auschwitz," 200.

69 Ibid., 191.

70 See, for instance, Theodor W. Adorno, "Philosophy and Teachers," in *Critical Models: Interventions and Catchwords* (New York: Columbia University Press, 1998): 19-36.

71 Peter Uwe Hohendahl, *Prismatic Thought: Theodor Adorno* (Lincoln, Nebraska: University of Nebraska Press, 1995): 58.

72 Some might argue that I am putting forward a view of Adorno that is too optimistic. But I think that Adorno's political pessimism, which, given his own experience of fascism, seems entirely justified to me, should not be confused with his pedagogical optimism, which provides some insight into why he could write the Auschwitz essay in the first place. Even Adorno's ambivalence around about what education could actually accomplish does not amount to an unadulterated pessimism as much as a caution regarding the limits of education as an emancipatory politics. Adorno wanted to make sure that individuals recognized those larger structures of power outside traditional appeals to education while clinging to critical thought as the precondition, but not absolute condition, of individual and social agency. I want to thank Larry Grossberg for this distinction. I also want to thank Roger Simon and Imre Szeman for their insightful comments on Adorno's politics and pessimism.

73 On the relationship between prisons and schools, see Giroux, *The Terror of Neoliberalism* (Boulder, CO: Paradigm, 2004).

74 Henry A. Giroux and Susan Searls Giroux, *Take Back Higher Education* (New York: Palgrave, 2004).

75 On the intellectual diversity issue, see Donald Lazere, "The Contradictions of Cultural Conservatism in the Assault on American Colleges," *Chronicle of Higher Education* (July 2, 2004): B15-B16.

76 Michael Collins Piper, "Schools Not Teaching Pro-Israel Views to Lose Funding: Congress to Pass 'Ideological Diversity' Legislation," *American Free Press* (April 22, 2003). Available on-line: http://www.picosearch.com/cgi-bin/ts.pl.

77 I want to thank my colleague and good friend, Sophia McClennen, for some of these ideas that emerged out of a personal e-mail correspondence on November 22, 2004.

78 For an example of how this type of authoritarianism works in the name of academic freedom, see Jennifer Jacobson, "A Liberal Professor Fights a Label," *The Chronicle of Higher Education* 51, no.14 (November 26, 2004): A8.

171

79 Adorno, "Education after Auschwitz," 192.

80 Ibid., 194.

81 Ibid., 196.

82 Ibid., 197-198.

83 George Smith refers to one program in which a woman was tied up in a clear box while some eager males "dumped a few hundred tarantulas onto her … you can hear the screaming and crying from her and the witnesses. Some guy is vomiting. This is critical, because emptying the contents of the stomach is great TV. Everyone else is laughing and smirking, just like our good old boys and girls at Abu Ghraib." George Smith, "That's Entrail-Tainment!" *The Village Voice*, August 3, 2004. Available online: www.villagevoice.com/isues/0431/essay.php.

84 This paragraph draws almost directly from a correspondence with Zygmunt Bauman, dated August 31, 2004.

85 Cited in Carol Becker, "The Art of Testimony," *Sculpture* (March 1997), 28.

86 Adorno, "Education after Auschwitz," 201.

87 This issue is taken up with great insight and compassion in Robert Jay Lifton, *Super Power Syndrome: America's Apocalyptic Confrontation with the World* (New York: Thunder Mouth Press, 2003).

88 Akeel Bilgrami, Forward to *Humanism and Democratic Criticism*, by Edward Said (New York: Columbia, 2004): x.

89 Adorno, "Education after Auschwitz," transcript of Radio Version (April 1966). Available on-line: www.chemtrailcentral.com/ubb/Forum6/HTML/001718.

90 I take up this issue in great detail in Henry A. Giroux, *Public Spaces, Private Lives: Democracy Beyond 9/11* (Lanham, MD.: Rowman and Littlefield, 2003).

91 One of the best books examining this issue is Robert W. McChesney, *Rich Media, Poor Democracy* (New York: The New Press, 1999).

92 Zygmunt Bauman, *In Search of Politics* (Stanford: Stanford University Press, 1999).

93 See Kevin Phillips, *Wealth and Democracy* (New York: Broadway Books, 2003).

94 Constructions of the impoverished other have a long history in American society, including more recent manifestations that extend from the internment of Japanese Americans during World War II to the increasing incarceration of young black and brown men in 2004. Of course, these constructions cannot be explained entirely within the discourse of capitalist relations. The fatal combination of chauvinism, mili-

tarism, and racism has produced an extensive history of photographic images in which depraved representations, such as blacks hanging from trees or skulls of "Japanese soldiers jammed onto a tank exhaust pipe as a trophy," depict a xenophobia far removed from the dictates of objectified consumerism. See John Louis Lucaites and James P. McDaniel, "Telescopic Mourning/Warring in the Global Village: Decomposing (Japanese) Authority Figures," *Communication and Critical/Cultural Studies* 1, no.1 (March 2004): 4. Also see Zygmunt Bauman, *Wasted Lives* (Cambridge, England: Polity Press, 2004).

95 Cornel West, "Finding Hope in Dark Times," *Tikkun* 19, no.4 (2004), 19-20.

96 William D. Hartung, "Outsourcing Is Hell," *The Nation* (June 7, 2004), 5.

97 Louis Navaer, "Terrorist Mercenaries on U.S. Payroll in Iraq War," *Pacific News Service*, May 4, 2004. Available on-line: www.mindfully.org/Reform/2004/Terrorist-Mercenaries-US4may04.htm.

98 Tim Shorrok, "CACI and Its Friends," *The Nation* (June 21, 2004), 22.

99 Ibid.

100 Nick Couldry, "In the Place of a Common Culture, What?" *The Review of Education, Pedagogy, and Cultural Studies* 26, no.1 (January-March 2004), 15.

101 Martha C. Nussbaum, "Compassion and Terror," *Daedalus* (Winter 2003): 11.

102 Adorno, "Education after Auschwitz," 203.

103 Janadas Devan, " The Rise of the Neo Conservatives," *The Straits Times* (March 30, 2004). Available on-line: www.straitstimes.asia1.com.sg/columnist/0,1886,145-180171-,00.html.

104 See for instance, Niall Ferguson, *Colossus: The Price of America's Empire* (New York: The Penguin Press, 2004); Michael Ignatieff, *The Lesser Evil: Political Ethics in an Age of Terror* (Princeton: Princeton University Press, 2004).

105 See Marc Cooper, "Dissing the Republic to Save It: A Conversation with Chalmers Johnson," *LA Weekly* (July 2-8, 2004). Available on-line: www.commondreams.org/views04/0701-2htm.

106 Said, *Humanism and Democratic Criticism*, 6.

107 William Greider, "Under the Banner of the 'War' on Terror," *The Nation* (June 21, 2004), 18.

108 Judith Butler, *Precarious Life: The Powers of Mourning and Violence* (London: Verso, 2004), 151.

109 This issue is taken up brilliantly in Zygmunt Bauman, *Wasted Lives: Modernity and Its*

Outcasts (London: Polity Press, 2004).

110 Butler, *Precarious Life*, xviii.

111 I want to illustrate this point with a comment taken from an Israeli soldier about his experience in Hebron:

I was ashamed of myself the day I realized that I simply enjoy the feeling of power. I don't believe in it: I think this is not the way to do anything to anyone, surely not to someone who has done nothing to you, but you can't help but enjoy it. People do what you tell them. You know it's because you carry a weapon. Knowing that if you didn't have it, and if your fellow soldiers weren't beside you, they would jump on you, beat the shit out of you, and stab you to death—you're beginning to enjoy it. Not merely enjoy it, you need it. And then, when someone suddenly says "No" to you, "What do you mean, no? Where do you draw the chutzpah from, to say no to me?" ... I remember a very specific situation: I was at a checkpoint, a temporary one, a so-called strangulation checkpoint, it was a very small checkpoint, very intimate, four soldiers, no commanding officer, no protection worthy of the name, a true moonlighting job, blocking the entrance to a village. From one side a line of cars wanting to get out, and from the other side a line of cars wanting to pass, a huge line, and suddenly you have a mighty force at the tip of your fingers, as if playing a computer game. I stand there like this, pointing at someone, gesturing to you to do this or that, and you do this or that, the car starts, moves toward me, halts beside me. The next car follows, you signal, it stops. You start playing with them, like a computer game. You come here, you go there, like this. You barely move, you make them obey the tip of your finger. It's a might feeling. It's something you don't experience elsewhere. You know it's because you have a weapon, you know it's because you are a soldier, you know all this, but it's addictive. When I realized this ... I checked in with myself to see what had happened to me. That's it. And it was a big bubble that burst. I thought I was immune, that is, how can someone like me, a thinking, articulate, ethical, moral man—things I can attest to about myself as such. Suddenly, I notice that I am getting addicted to controlling people.

I want to thank Roger Simon for this insight and for his making available to me the transcript from which this quote is taken. See "Soldiers Speak Out about Their Service in Hebron." Available on-line at www.shovrimshtika.org.

3

WHEN HOPE IS SUBVERSIVE

Is it possible to imagine hope for justice and humanity after the abuse, rape, and torture of children and other Iraqi detainees by American soldiers at Abu Ghraib prison? What does hope mean when the United States, as the most powerful nation in the world, is virtually unchallenged at home in incarcerating unprecedented numbers of young people of colour? What does hope teach us at a time in which government lies and deception are exposed daily in the media and yet appear to have little effect on President Bush's popular support? What does hope offer in resisting a government that abducts people and sends them to authoritarian countries to be tortured? What resources and visions does hope offer in a society in which greed is considered venerable and profit is the most important measure of personal achievement and social advance? What is the relevance of hope at a time when most attempts to interrupt the operations of an incipient fascism appear to fuel a growing cynicism rather than promote widespread individual and collective acts of resistance?

These questions point to the growing sense that politics in American life has become corrupt, progressive social change a distant memory, and hope the last refuge of deluded romantics, especially in light of the overt turn toward authoritarianism marked by the re-election of George W. Bush in 2004. Those traditional public spheres in which people could exchange ideas, debate, and shape the conditions that structured their everyday lives increasingly appear to have little substance—where they still exist—let alone political importance. Civic engagement seems irrelevant and democratic public values are rendered invisible in light of the growing power of multinational corporations to privatize public space and time as they disconnect power from issues of equity, social justice, and civic responsibility. Political exhaustion and impoverished intellectual visions are fed by the widely popular assumption that there are no alternatives to the present state of affairs. As Lewis Lapham points out, the right-wing and neoliberal propaganda mill endlessly grinds out the news that any vestige of the public, whether it be public service, public health, public goods, public life, or public schools, is either hopelessly inefficient or simply a relic of Satanic socialism.[1] And the dumbing down of public discourse takes a toll on civic culture. For instance, a recent survey of 112,003 students found that "36% believe newspapers should get government approval of stories before publishing" and another 32% claim that the "press enjoys too much freedom."[2] This disregard for democracy, the retreat from social justice, and a rampaging anti-intellectualism are further amplified by the increasing corporatization of everyday life and the consequent predominance of market values over social values. One consequence is that people with the education and means appear more and more willing to retreat into the safe, privatized enclaves of the family, religion, and consumption, while those without the luxury of such choices pay a terrible price in what Zygmunt Bauman calls the "hard currency of human suffering."[3]

Unlike some theorists who suggest that politics as a site of contestation, critical exchange, and engagement has either come to an end or is in a state of terminal arrest, I believe that the current depressing state of politics points to the urgent challenge of reformulating the crisis of democracy as part of the fundamental crisis of vision, meaning, education, and political agency. Politics devoid of vision either degenerates into cynicism or appropriates a view of power equated with domination. Lost from such accounts is the recognition that democracy has to be struggled over—even in the face of a most appalling crisis of educational opportunity and political agency. There is also too little attention paid to the fact that the struggle over politics and democracy is inextricably linked to creating and sustaining public spheres where individuals can be engaged as political agents equipped with the skills, capacities, and knowledge they need not only to actually perform as autonomous political agents, but also to believe that such struggles are worth taking up. It also means taking back people's time in an era when the majority must work more than they ever have to make ends meet. The growth of cynicism in American society may say less about the reputed apathy of the populace than it does about the bankruptcy of the old political languages and the need for a new language and vision for clarifying intellectual, ethical and political projects, especially as they work to reframe questions of agency and meaning for a substantive democracy.

Yet crafting a new political language requires what I call "educated hope." Hope, in this instance, is the precondition for individual and social struggle, involving the ongoing practice of critical education in a wide variety of sites and the renewal of civic courage among citizens who wish to address pressing social problems. In this sense, educated hope is a subversive force. In opposition to those who seek to turn hope into a new slogan, or who punish and dismiss efforts to look beyond the horizon of the given, progressives need to resurrect a language of resistance and possibility, a language in which hope is viewed as both a project and a pedagogical condition for providing a sense of opposition and engaged struggle. As a project, Andrew Benjamin insists, hope must be viewed as "a structural condition of the present rather than as the promise of a future, the continual promise of a future that will always have to have been better."[4] Rather than viewed as an individual proclivity, hope must be seen as part of a broader politics that acknowledges those social, economic, spiritual, and cultural conditions in the present that make certain kinds of agency and democratic politics possible.[5]

The philosopher Ernst Bloch provides essential theoretical insights on the importance of hope. He argues that hope must be concrete, a spark that reaches out beyond the surrounding emptiness of capitalist relations, anticipating a better world in the future, a world that speaks to us by presenting tasks based on the challenges of the present time. For Bloch, hope becomes concrete when it links the possibility of the "not yet" with forms of political agency animated by a determined effort to engage critically with the past and present in order to address pressing social problems and realizable tasks.[6] Bloch believes that hope cannot be removed from the world and is not "something like nonsense or absolute fancy; rather it is not yet in the sense of a possibility; that it could be there if we could only do something for it."[7] As a discourse of critique and social transformation, hope in Bloch's view foregrounds the crucial relationship between critical education and political agency, on the one hand, and the concrete struggles needed to give substance to the recognition that every present is incomplete, on the other. For theorists such as Bloch and his more contemporary counterparts such as Cornel West and Robin D.G. Kelley, hope is anticipatory rather than messianic, mobilizing rather than therapeutic. The longing for a more humane society in this instance does not collapse into a retreat from the world, but emerges out of critical and practical engagements with present behaviours, institutional formations, and everyday practices. Hope in this context does not ignore the worse dimensions of human suffering, exploitation, and social relations; on the contrary, it acknowledges the need to sustain the "capacity to see the worst and offer more than that for our consideration."[8]

Hence, hope is more than a politics; it is also a pedagogical and performative practice that provides the foundation for enabling human beings to learn about their potential as moral and civic agents. Hope is the outcome of those pedagogical practices and struggles that tap into memory and lived experiences while at the same time linking individual responsibility with a progressive sense of social change. As a form of utopian longing, educated hope opens up horizons of comparison by evoking not just different histories, but different futures. At the same time, it substantiates the importance of ambivalence and problematizes certainty or, as Paul Ricoeur has suggested, it is "a major resource as the weapon against closure."⁹ Educated hope is a subversive force when it pluralizes politics by opening up a space for dissent, making authority accountable, and becoming an activating presence in promoting social transformation.

The current limits of the utopian imagination are related, in part, to the failure of progressives to imagine what pedagogical conditions might be necessary to bring into being forms of political agency that might expand the operations of individual rights, social provisions, and democratic freedoms. At the same time, a politics and pedagogy of hope is neither a blueprint for the future nor a form of social engineering, but a belief, simply, that different futures are possible, holding open matters of contingency, context, and indeterminacy. It is only through critical forms of education that human beings can learn about the limits of the present and the conditions necessary to "combine a gritty sense of limits with a lofty vision of possibility."¹⁰ Educated hope poses the important challenge of how to reclaim social agency within a broader struggle to deepen the possibilities for social justice and global democracy. This position is echoed by Judith Butler, who argues, "For me there is more hope in the world when we can question what is taken for granted, especially about what it is to be human."[11] Zygmunt Bauman goes further, arguing that the resurrection of any viable notion of political and social agency is dependent upon a culture of questioning, whose purpose, as he puts it, is to "keep the forever unexhausted and unfulfilled human potential open, fighting back all attempts to foreclose and preempt the further unravelling of human possibilities, prodding human society to go on questioning itself and preventing that questioning from ever stalling or being declared finished."[12]

Reclaiming politics is a pedagogical practice and performative act. It requires a form of educated hope that accentuates how politics is played out on the terrain of imagination and desire as well as in material relations of power and concrete social formations. Freedom and justice, in this instance, have to be mediated through the connection between civic education and political agency, which presupposes that the goal of educated hope is not to liberate the individual from the social—a central tenet of neoliberalism—but to take seriously the notion that the individual can only be liberated through the social. Educated hope, as a subversive, defiant practice, should provide a link, however transient, provisional, and contextual, between vision and critique, on the one hand, and engagement and transformation, on the other. But for such a notion of hope to be consequential, it has to be grounded in a pedagogical project that has some hold on the present. Hope becomes meaningful to the degree that it identifies agencies and processes, offers alternatives to an age of profound pessimism, reclaims an ethic of compassion and justice, and contends for those institutions in which equality, freedom, and justice flourish as part of the ongoing struggle for a global democracy.

1   Lewis Lapham, "Tentacles of Rage: The Republican Propaganda Mill, A Brief History," *Harper's* (September 2004), 41.

2   Greg Toppo, "U.S. Students Say Press Freedoms Go Too Far," *USA Today* (January 31, 2004). Available on-line: www.commondreams.org/cgi-bin/print.cgi?file=/headlines050131-02.htm.

3   Zygmunt Bauman, *Globalization: The Human Consequences* (New York: Columbia University Press, 1998): 5.

4   Andrew Benjamin, *Present Hope: Philosophy, Architecture, Judaism* (New York: Routledge, 1997): 1.

5   Henry A. Giroux, *Public Spaces, Private Lives: Democracy Beyond 9/11* (Lanham: Rowman and Littlefield, 2002).

6   Ernst Bloch's great contribution in English on the subject of utopianism can be found in his three-volume work, *The Principle of Hope,* trans. Neville Plaice, Stephen Plaice, and Paul Knight (1959; Cambridge: MIT Press, 1986).

7   Ernst Bloch, "Something's Missing: A Discussion between Ernst Bloch and Theodor W. Adorno on the Contradictions of Utopia Longing," in Ernst Bloch, *The Utopian Function of Art and Literature: Selected Essays* (Cambridge, MA: MIT Press, 1988): 3.

8   Thomas L. Dunn, "Political Theory for Losers," in *Vocations of Political Theory,* ed. Jason A. Frank and John Tambornino (Minneapolis: University of Minnesota Press, 2000): 160.

9   Cited in Zygmunt Bauman, *Work, Consumerism and the New Poor* (Philadelphia: Open University Press, 1998): 98.

10 Ron Aronson, "Hope after Hope?" *Social Research* 66, no.2 (Summer 1999): 489.

11 Cited in Gary A. Olson and Lynn Worsham, "Changing the Subject: Judith Butler's Politics of Radical Resignification," *JAC* 20, no.4 (2000), 765.

12 Zygmunt Bauman and Keith Tester, *Conversations with Zygmunt Bauman* (Malden, MA: Polity Press, 2001): 4.

4

RETHINKING POLITICS, EDUCATION, AND
HOPE AFTER BUSH

Henry A. Giroux, a leading figure in the fields of critical pedagogy and cultural studies, recently came to McMaster University in Canada from Penn State University, where he taught for more than a decade. He is the author of more than 30 books and 250 journal articles. He was interviewed by Sina Rahmani in his office at McMaster.

Sina Rahmani: Your leaving Penn State was not exactly amicable. You commented that the intellectual atmosphere at Penn State had degraded in recent years. Is that related at all to the current state of affairs of American political culture?

Henry Giroux: I think that many universities in the United States are being undermined by both their increasing alliance with corporate values and interests, on the one hand, and the equally dangerous attack on academic freedom by the political and religious Right, on the other hand. We have witnessed four years in the United States marked by a growing culture of fear, insecurity, and repression. This is a culture largely controlled by religious, political, and free-market fundamentalists; this combination, and the power it has exercised on American life, has been profoundly dangerous. The current government is involved in a war at home and a war abroad, both of which are mediated by a messianic view of the world that does not leave much room for dissent, nor for social movements that want to make authority accountable or forms of public and higher education that act as if they are democratic public spheres. And, of course, with Bush's re-election this will all get worse. The Bush administration views higher education as a left-wing bastion that needs to be destroyed, and I am convinced that in his second administration, the universities will continue to come under a harsh political attack. At the same time, the right-wing attack on critical intellectuals offers the Bush administration the kinds of diversions that sidetrack people from thinking about the Iraq war, the resources it is draining, the lives being lost, and the suffering it is producing. We have seen remnants of the attack on higher education already with many academics after the events of September 11th being called "unpatriotic" because they undertook a serious examination of American foreign policy or called "anti-Semitic" because they dared criticize the Israeli government's policies in the Middle East. A senator from Pennsylvania even tried to pass a law withdrawing federal funds from those public universities that harboured professors who criticized Israeli policy in their classes. These are very disturbing trends and do not bode well as to what will happen in higher education in the next four years. So, we are seeing a new war, a war at home, and that war will basically be against the universities. We already see the indications of how that war is going to be organized. We see it in the unjust association made between dissent and treason. We see it in legislation in which Republicans, through an appeal to academic freedom, attempt to place more conservatives on faculties. We see it in the increasing corporatization of the university and the marginalization of those disciplines that don't translate immediately into profits. Penn State is one of the largest procurers of military contractors. Susan Searls Giroux and I had written a book called *Take Back Higher Education* on the corporatization of higher education. Essentially, it is an attack on the corporate university, of which Penn State is a poster boy. There was no question in my mind that there would be retribution, though I never anticipated the shape it actually took. What became clear was that Penn State had become inhospitable to any kind of dissent. To be an academic and to constantly find yourself under pressure and isolated, by virtue of an atmosphere of anti-intellectualism and conformity, was completely unacceptable for me. It was a pleasure for me to leave.

SR: Why McMaster? World-class scholar and educator, you could have gone anywhere. Why a small, out-of-the-way school like Mac?

HG: Well, I think McMaster is improving upon its goal of becoming a world-class institution. And I don't just mean that in the traditional sense of attaining the standards of research, teaching, and academic excellence that one associates with Ivy League schools in the United States. Surely, McMaster is capable of attaining the highest quality of excellence in the traditional sense, but I think it is also providing a new model of excellence, one that measures a university in terms of how it addresses the needs of civic society on both national and global levels. McMaster takes seriously the relationship between equity and excellence as a political and civic issue. There is a certain worldliness about McMaster, a sense of being in the world, being attentive to the civic quality of a larger, global public sphere. This means, in part, taking seriously what it means to educate students to be critically engaged, civic citizens of the world. Worldliness, as I am using it here, means recognizing the university as a democratic public sphere, a sphere that not only acknowledges the importance of educating students to exercise civic courage and define their lives, in part, through the struggle for social justice and the deepening of democratic imperatives, but also takes seriously the relationship between education and empowerment. This is a university that recruits faculty who combine the contemplative and critical with a broader sense of the importance of public life. It's recruiting faculty who are not afraid to speak out, take risks, cross disciplines, and at the same time create a common symbolic space aimed at fostering more inclusive democratic communities. They really see their role as one of promoting a very viable and crucial public service. Closer to my own location in the university, I see McMaster working very hard to provide a new face for the Humanities. That is, a Humanities that is not just about enlightenment, in the traditional sense of the term—critical yet utterly contemplative—but is also about preparing students to intervene in public life so as to expand and deepen the possibilities of a global democracy. I think this is a Humanities that resurrects the best of its critical traditions while at the same time using those traditions, along with the development of new technologies, information systems, and interdisciplinary crossings to define the university as a public sphere, essential to sustaining a vibrant democracy and to help educate students who will be the individual and social agents central to such a challenge. A vibrant university fulfils its public role when it provides the institutional and symbolic resources necessary for young people to develop their capacities to engage in critical thought, participate in power relations and policy decisions that affect their lives, and transform those racial, social, and economic inequities that close down democratic social relations. We have a Dean of the Humanities, Nasrin Rahimieh, who is very smart, brave, and visionary. I really think she needs to be commended for that. In my thirty years, I haven't met very many visionary administrators, and there are more than a handful at McMaster, and I am grateful for her courage and intellectual integrity. We have a growing number of faculty throughout the university who are thinking very thoughtfully about the rapid developments in science, technology, culture, and globalization, as well as the ethical and political implications and the global effects of these changes. We have faculty such as Imre Szeman, David Clark, Liss Platt, Sarah Brophy, Susie O'Brien, and too many others to mention, throughout the university who are doing impressive cross-cutting interdisciplinary work in areas such as critical theory, gender studies, cultural studies, global studies, and communication, and I have no doubt that their insights will broaden and enhance the scholarship that goes on within the traditional disciplines. McMaster seems to have taken on the challenge of recruiting faculty who are offering a range of critical literacies, civic competencies, technological skills, and ethical values that serve the noble purpose of improving what some people have called the larger, global public sphere.

SR: The stereotype that seems to pervade public life about academics is that they are detached eggheads with no connection to the world outside. What role do you envisage yourself as playing for students at McMaster?

HG: I think professors and academics in general have a number of obligations to students. On one level, there is the obligation to bring into play a body of knowledge that helps to expand their sense of social and individual agency. It's an obligation, in a sense, to make students more aware of the world in which they find themselves. This suggests educating students to learn how to be able to live in an inclusive and non-repressive democracy. It means nurturing those capacities that enable them to take risks, to make democratic politics and public commitments central to their lives. For me, that obligation does not simply rest on expanding the boundaries of knowledge and skills for students, as important as such a goal is. It also rests on making students more aware of how knowledge can be used as a social, intellectual, and theoretical resource to make them more responsible as agents who can actively shape the larger world. It means using knowledge in more than a narrowly instrumental way—such as preparing for a job—it also means critically embracing knowledge as a means of self-development tied to modes of learning and intellectual work that address matters of human freedom, equality, and social justice. Learning in this instance is linked not just to understanding, but also to social change, to those modes of moral witnessing necessary to transform the underlying systemic conditions that produce human suffering. It seems to me that my obligation, in the long run, is to prepare students for a very complex and contradictory world, in which they are going to learn how to govern and not simply be governed. At the same time, they will, I hope, associate their own sense of self-determination and agency with modes of governance that are democratic, cosmopolitan, and deeply concerned with matters of economic and social justice. I may be terribly wrong on this issue, but I think academics have to ask themselves very crucial questions about their vision of the future, their responsibilities as citizens, the role of the state and government, and what the responsibility of the university might be in terms of its liberatory functions.

SR: You bring up the issue of dissent. What do you see as the role of an oppositional academic?

HG: The role of the oppositional academic is essentially to make power accountable, and to do everything one can, both in one's teaching and research, to make clear to students the political and moral stakes about what it might mean to contribute to a culture and social order in which human suffering goes unnoticed and actually becomes normalized. So it seems to me that, as an intellectual, you have a responsibility by virtue of your resources, not to mention the division of labour that academics inhabit, to enter into a discourse in which you can make power visible, and employ a language of critique and possibility to enable students to recognize that they can be important political actors in shaping the world they inherit. Central to any viable education is the ability to translate private issues into public concerns, to use theory as a resource and hope as a pedagogical tool to look beyond the horizon of the given, to mediate the memory of loss and the experience of injustice as part of a broader attempt to open up new locations of struggle and undermine various forms of injustice and domination. We live in a world in which educators have a responsibility to rethink the space of the social and to develop a critical language in which notions of the public good and public life become central to overcoming the privatizing and depoliticizing language of the market. Academics must address the subversive role of the university, its role in preventing institutions from governing without being challenged. Clearly, as public intellectuals, academics can, as Edward Said has suggested, temper any reverence for authority with a sense of critical awareness. Students must engage new modes of literacy in which, to read the world, they must be both critics and cultural producers; they must be able to recognize anti-democratic assaults on public life; and they need a language to defend those vital institutions that are central to every aspect of democratic life. They also need to learn how to read the world from the perspectives of those victims of "democracy" who have their own lessons to teach about what it means to live in a global democracy. I think Jacques Derrida was right in arguing that the university should be a place of unconditional resistance, a place in which nothing is beyond question. At one level, this points to the need for academics to beware of the pitfalls of specialization and professionalism, which often substitute a professional vocation for an intellectual vocation. Professionalism has more to do with reverence than critique, with careerism than an engagement with public life. At the same time, I think that academics must take seriously the presupposition that the task of pedagogy, in the most critical sense, is about critically engaging how knowledge, values, desire, and social relations are implicated in power. Academics must recognize that pedagogy is a moral and political practice, and not merely a methodology, and that it is always an outcome of struggles and cannot be viewed as an a priori discourse that simply needs to be uncovered or revealed. Pedagogy is not just a struggle over particular forms of knowledge or identities; it is also a struggle over how one views the future and what it might mean to prepare students to imagine not only a different future, but one that makes a claim on social justice, solidarity, and the promise of an inclusive democracy.

SR: Where is the best place to do that kind of work? As an American, how do you feel about your role as a critical intellectual being played out in Canada? What responsibilities flow from being a dissenting American?

HG: Being in Canada is a humbling experience for me because I have to learn about the diverse histories, politics, and traditions that inform my current location. At the same time, what I write about is not limited by national boundaries because much of my work on youth, higher education, critical pedagogy, cultural studies, etc., has relevance on a broader, global level. But what Canada offers me in the more pragmatic, if not political, sense is a place that is far more hospitable to the kind of political and educational work that has shaped my life. More importantly, it offers me a community of people to work collaboratively with; it provides an environment that encourages critical thought and refuses to indulge the poisonous intolerance that guides policy at the highest level of government in the United States; and it encourages academic work that engages public life. Good intellectual work never takes place in a vacuum; it is always communal, social, vibrant, and draws upon many voices and dialogues. This is a difficult space to create within the university for a variety of reasons ranging from professionalism to sheer petty careerism, but McMaster is a different place for me and provides a space that is more hospitable to community, experimentation, and critical, productive work. Such work always emerges from a community of people who support you and from whom you learn. What I have here, as opposed to what I had at Penn State, is a community that is fabulous. Even my students are wonderful. They are smart, open, involved, and they have a sense of being in the world. I feel renewed in this environment. You can't romanticize critical work in the form of the isolated intellectual performing an endless Sisyphean task. There is nothing romantic about working alone without a sense of community. The romanticization of the isolated intellectual is just that—romanticizing—and I find that McMaster offers a different model for what it means to invent new modes of academic solidarity and active collaborations across disciplines, and to work within new and challenging interdisciplinary contexts.

AGAINST THE NEW AUTHORITARIANISM

SR: What do foresee in the next four years for your American colleagues?

HG: I think the next four years are going to be a very dangerous time for people who are critical academics. I think we are going to enter into a period of enormous repression in the United States.

SR: Some would argue that we already have.

HG: I am not suggesting it doesn't exist now—I have talked about it earlier—but I think it is going to intensify to point where it may be difficult to protect those spaces that traditionally were by default, safe, critical, and conducive to the spirit of engaged teaching and academic freedom. New assaults against tenure are in the works, along with increasing attempts to dictate what is being taught, to standardize the undergraduate curriculum, to eliminate those non-instrumental courses that are increasingly viewed as ornamental, and to hire administrators who are managers but not leaders or visionaries. We may also see new attacks on people who express dissident views by attempting to run them out of the university.

SR: That's already happening in Middle Eastern studies.

HG: You're correct, and I think that process will be generalized. We see it happening at Columbia with Joseph Massad, who is under terrific attack because every time he utters a critique of Israel, he's called an anti-Semite. I think these kinds of attacks will increase in the United States in the next few years so that anyone who takes a critical position will be labelled as either un-American or unpatriotic. This attack on dissent is already having a terrible chilling effect throughout higher education in the US, and will continue to reinforce a landscape of fear and intimidation that is already a staple of the larger society. People will be very scared about losing their jobs, careers, livelihood, and sense of agency. The current attacks on Ward Churchill, Joseph Massad, and others exemplify the attack by the Right on academic freedom. This trend is very disturbing but not surprising, given the extremists who now control almost all branches of the American government. That's disturbing and frightening.

SR: How do you think students are going to respond to such an atmosphere?

HG: I see enormous movements of opposition developing in the US in the next four years. These movements will build on existing movements and will create new social formations as well. I think you're going to see a substantial amount of collective resistance by students who are not going to tolerate this push to conformity, repression, and the mindless drive of American triumphalism. Many on the Right believe that the universities embody the worst excesses of democracy. Students will not stand for the attack on academic freedom, the increasing corporatization of the university, a national debt that will ruin their future, the assault on public life, the colonial march of empire, the suspension of civil liberties, the rise of a surveillance and control society, and the shrinking of democracy itself. All this spells more dissent and more student protests. The resistance of students is all the more necessary in the face of so much silence by academics, unions, and other progressive adults.

SR: You seem to suggest that the US is going back to the Middle Ages.

HG: No, not the Middle Ages. The Gilded Age is more like it. That period in American history when the robber barons and politicians worked together to limit workers' rights, maintain a racialized state, keep women in their place, and reduce every transaction to one of profit and exchange. Power has become arrogant as the new political structures being invented by the Right barely feel the need to legitimate themselves. Hence, people like Samuel Huntington now publish books in which they make overtly racist remarks about Mexicans. Then, there are the public relations, intellectual buffoons such as Ann Coulter, Rush Limbaugh, and that crew, who provide an endless discourse of hate, bigotry, and bile.

SR: And why should we worry about these people?

HG: Because they not only drive policy, they play an important role in shaping public culture and individual consciousness. Ideas matter. And these people have access to enormous amounts of power and influence, and use it to drown out dissenting opinions, which are rarely expressed in the dominant media. Academia is considered dangerous by the Right because it is one of the few public spheres left where debate, dialogue, and critical engagement can actually take place.

SR: Is Bush's re-election a failure on the part of progressive academics?

HG: It may testify less to our failure than to the strengths of neo-conservatives, religious fundamentalists, and free-market extremists. Remember, they control the means of educational production. They control the universities and, for the most part, those dominant spaces where ideas can be produced, legitimated, and circulated. I think it means that progressive academics have to rethink not simply their own role as public intellectuals, but also what it might mean to develop a language and theory relevant for inventing a politics adequate to the challenges of the twenty-first century. Intellectuals across the globe have got to bring their resources together, develop new alliances, and begin to play a powerful role in shaping political culture. We also need to be more concerned about working with groups outside the university. We have to rethink the meaning of politics in the twenty-first century because there is no space outside politics. To assume that somehow politics is absent from what we do may be comforting for some but, in the end, it is one of the worst illusions.

SR: Can your emphasis on politics be dangerous?

HG: Any issue can succumb to forms of dogmatism. Anybody who considers themself a critical intellectual has to be constantly aware of the dangers that can be produced in the name of politics. Simply to say that we are political is not an excuse for dogmatism. The real question here is, how do we refashion politics in way that resuscitates its democratic possibilities?

Index

INDEX

INDEX

INDEX

INDEX

INDEX

INDEX

philosophy, 94; and politics, 82-3, 94; and poverty, 83, 86; and proto-fascism, 37, 85, 94; and public good, 86, 91; and public services, 86; and public spheres, 85, 86, 91, 92; and punishment, 94; and social contract, 94; and state, 83, 87-8, 93; in US, 84, 86-7; and welfare state, 83, 84

New Deal, 4, 38

The New Republic, 28n.54

New Right, 36-7

Newspeak, 47, 49-50, 52

New York Daily News, 52

New Yorker, 113

New York Times, 70, 120

Nichols, John, 45, 46

Niger, uranium from, 52

9/11. See September 11th, 2001

1984 (Orwell), 50, 51, 94

No Child Left Behind Act, 43, 68

Norquist, Grover, 48-9

North Korea, 15

Northrop Grumman, 154

NOW, 47

Obama, Barack, 158

Olin Foundation, 7, 10

O'Neill, Paul, 99n.35

Orwell, George: *1984*, 50, 94

other(s), 149-50, 153, 163

outsourcing, 84, 153

Paige, Rod, 43-4, 56

paintball, 76

Parker, Kathleen, 8

patriotism, 7, 18, 41-2; and Abu Ghraib abuses, 134, 150; and criticism, 124, 130; and dissent, 124; and fashion, 80; and higher education, 185; profits from, 79; and social policies, 152

Paxton, Robert, 35-6

pedagogy, 192; and Abu Ghraib abuses, 133-4; and critical citizenry, 135; as ethical practice, 136; and hope, 179-80, 191; inhumanity and, 136-7; and justice, 162; and politics, 136; sites of, 75-6, 95, 129-30, 131, 133, 135, 136, 141, 148, 155, 156, 161; and translation of images, 134-5. *See also* education; public pedagogy

Penn State University, 184, 186, 193

Pentagon, 12-13, 17, 77, 91, 116

people of colour: civil rights of, 69; incarceration of, 73, 93, 115, 175; in US, 32-3, 175. *See also* African Americans

Perle, Richard, 157

photographs, 128-9; of Abu Ghraib abuses, 110-12, 120-1, 128-30, 131, 133; as forms of public pedagogy, 130-2; and power, 129, 132; reading of, 129, 132

INDEX

INDEX

INDEX

INDEX